THE

COOKBOOK

THE

WHITE LILY

A Southern Tradition Since 1883

COOKBOOK

*A Collection of Recipes Using the
Southern Chef's Flour of Choice*

Copyright © 2021 by Hometown Food Company

WHITE LILY, WHITE LILY SINCE 1883, and WHITE LILY A SOUTHERN TRADITION SINCE 1883 are registered trademarks and trademarks of Hometown Food Company in the United States and/or other countries.

The White Lily Flour product packaging is a copyright of Hometown Food Company.

All rights reserved. No part of this book may be reproduced or transmitted in any form or by any means, electronic or mechanical, including photocopying, or by any information storage and retrieval system, without permission in writing from 83 Press. Reviewers may quote brief passages for specific inclusion in a magazine or newspaper.

83 Press
2323 2nd Avenue North
Birmingham, AL 35203
hoffmanmedia.com

ISBN: 979-8-9913469-7-9
Printed in China

CONTENTS

8 FOREWORD

10 BISCUITS

34 CORNBREAD

54 SOUTHERN SUPPER STAPLES

74 CAKES

96 PIES & FRUIT DESSERTS

116 COOKIES & BARS

128 BREADS

150 FROM THE VAULT

FOREWORD

If you want to hear a Southerner indulge in a moment of nostalgia, just ask them to describe their momma's biscuits. A plate stacked with tender, hot, flaky biscuits has been the ultimate breakfast in the South since fine-textured, soft wheat flour and baking soda became available.

In fact, for a long time, biscuits were the only fast food in the South. Quick to make and easy to carry, they could sustain you through long days working in the fields, the mills, and wherever your work took you. They even made the perfect afternoon pick-me-up for school-children and parents alike.

It was the commercial development of baking powder and baking soda—as well as the availability of affordable flour from commercial mills—that gave rise to the South's reputation for light and tender biscuits. In 1883, J. Allen Smith reopened the Knoxville Mills in Tennessee. Not long after, bakers realized that the product that would come to be known as White Lily Flour was the perfect choice for making biscuits.

For years to come, cooks would use their hand-hewn wooden dough bowls to whip up batch after batch of biscuits for breakfast and dinner. The biscuit maker would first dip a heaping teacupful of flour from the barrel to the shallow, long, hollowed-out piece of tree trunk called a dough bowl. Then, a pile of flour would be swept to one end of the bowl, and salt, baking soda, and baking powder—the amounts gauged by touch alone—would be mixed in one by one. The baker would then work in the shortening, the tips of their fingers flying though the dry ingredients as they rubbed the mixture into flaky particles. Cold buttermilk would be poured in a little bit at a time—most families owned a cow or patronized a neighbor who sold milk and butter—and the mixture would be kneaded together. The dough would then be rolled out on a table lightly sprinkled with flour, and the biscuits would be cut before they were placed into a wood-fired cast-iron stove.

Today, homemade biscuits are more often a weekend treat than an everyday staple, but the comforting, soul-satisfying goods remain a timeless favorite. Though some of the mystique of making biscuits has gone the way of the dough bowl, the joy and excitement they bring to the table never fades. Once you've made a few batches of these beauties yourself, you'll never be able to fake out your family with canned biscuits again.

6-67

SHIPPING BAG
requirements of
FREIGHT CLASSIFICATION
rranteed by
ORGE COMPANY
SBURG, W. VA.

10 LBS.
NET

WHITE LILY

SELF-RISING

SELF-RISING FOR BAKING EASE
AND CONVENIENCE

10 LBS.
NET

WHITE LILY
FLOUR
ENRICHED · BLEACHED

Self-Rising

8 OZS. OF ENRICHED SELF-RISING
FLOUR SUPPLY NOT LESS THAN
THE FOLLOWING PROPORTIONS
OF THE MINIMUM DAILY RE-
QUIREMENTS OF: THIAMINE,
100%; RIBOFLAVIN, 50%; NIA-
CIN, 80%; CALCIUM, 33%; AND
IRON, 65%; THIAMINE, RIBO-
FLAVIN AND NIACIN ARE B
VITAMINS.

SELF-RISING FLOUR
PREPARED WITH SODA, PHOS-
PHATE LEAVENING AND SALT.
J. ALLEN SMITH & CO.
KNOXVILLE, TENNESSEE

WHITE LILY FLOUR
ENRICHED · BLE

BANANA LA
2¼ cups sifted Wh
Self-rising Flo
1¼ cups sugar
½ cup shortening
1½ cups mashed
(four or five)
2 eggs
1 teaspoon vani
Sift flour and sugar
bowl. Add shortenin
and eggs. Beat 2 m
speed. Add remainin
nilla, and beat 1 m
batter into grease
pans and bake
(375°F) about 25
done.

CHOCOLA
2 cups sifted W
Self-rising Flo
½ teaspoon salt
1½ teaspoons soc
½ cup shortenin
1½ cups sugar
2 eggs
2 squares choco
1 teaspoon vani
1 cup buttermi
Sift flour, salt, and
set aside. Melt c
double boiler. Crea
ually adding sugar
a time, mixing we
tion. Blend in cho
Alternately add
milk, mixing well,
lightly greased and
pans and bake
(350°F) for 30 to

Send
NEW COOK
BOO

16 pages of Treasu
It's free! For you

WHITE LILY KITCH
P. O. Box 871
Knoxville, Tennes

WHIT

CHAPTER 1

BISCUITS

Whether you're serving them up with butter and jam or ham and mustard, you just can't go wrong when you present your loved ones with a batch of biscuits. Classic, comforting, and crowd-pleasing, you'll be asked again and again, "What's your recipe?"

THE ESSENTIALS

Lower-Protein Flour

At White Lily, the wheat goes through a special milling process, and only the best 50 percent of the flour—called Fancy Patent Flour—is packaged and sold to home cooks, while the rest is sold to commercial bakeries. The milling process creates flour with a lighter volume. In fact, 1 cup plus 2 tablespoons White Lily Flour is equivalent to 1 cup flour from other brands. The high quality also means a brighter, whiter flour. You won't see the grayish-white color or the black specks that can be found in other brands of flour.

Low-protein flours like White Lily's all-purpose and self-rising flours are ideal for anything that needs to be tender, such as piecrusts, cakes, biscuits, and muffins. They're also perfect for quick breads, pancakes, sauces, and gravy. Most of these products are chemically leavened with baking powder and baking soda—both of which work in an entirely different way than yeast.

If you add hot water to baking powder, you will instantly see a great rush of fine bubbles. Strong sheets of gluten in high-protein flours actually interfere with this type of leavening by holding the mass of bubbles down. Low-protein flours have long been prized in Asia for making soft noodles and are also similar to Italian flour—some Italian chefs love it, plain or mixed with a little semolina, for pasta.

Higher-Protein Flour

The gluten in high-protein flours like White Lily's bread flour is ideal for yeast breads. Yeast oozes a liquid that releases carbon dioxide gas and alcohol to inflate tiny bubbles already in the dough. The elastic gluten sheets expand during the steady, gentle inflating process, and the dough rises.

The elastic sheets of gluten are strong and work to hold things together. If your cookies are crumbly, you need more gluten. If the tops come off your muffins, you need more gluten. You want strong gluten for pizza, some pastas, and strudel dough, and it must be stretched thin for puffed pastry, Danish, and croissants that must hold steam and puff apart.

Flour Finesse
There are three kinds of wheat flour you can buy at the grocery store: flour made from soft winter wheat grown in the South and Midwest, flour from the hard wheat of colder climates, and flour that's a mix of both soft and hard wheat.

Soft wheat flour makes the tender biscuits Southerners love. Hard wheat results in tough biscuits. Most national brand flours are a combination of hard and soft wheat. However, both White Lily All-Purpose Flour and White Lily Self-Rising Flour are 100-percent soft wheat flour.

FATS & LIQUIDS

Butter
Butter in baked goods provides moisture, tenderness, flakiness, and flavor. Use unsalted butter in baked goods so you can control the salt level.

Shortening
Shortening is a white flavorless fat made from vegetable oil. It is shelf-stable, less expensive, and easier to work with than butter, but it does not have the same flavor or richness. Baked goods made with shortening tend to rise higher, hold their shape while baking, and have a lighter interior texture.

Oil
Oil is a liquid fat most commonly made from vegetables. These types of oils, also called neutral oils, are preferred for baked goods since they do not have any strong flavors. The most common types are vegetable, canola, cottonseed, corn, and peanut; they can be used interchangeably.

Milk
Milk is classified by the milk fat it contains, which ranges from whole milk to fat-free (skim milk). Whole milk is usually preferred.

Buttermilk
Buttermilk is a milk with a heavier texture and distinctive taste. It adds a tangy but sweet taste to baked goods. Whole buttermilk is usually preferred, but you can use low-fat or non-fat buttermilk.

BISCUIT BASICS

Think you don't have anything to add in your biscuits? Think again!

CHEESE

CHIVES

BLUEBERRIES

While it's difficult to improve on White Lily's famous biscuits—they're the South's gold standard for a reason—there are fun ways to experiment with them and add extra flair. Here are some favorite add-ins to classic biscuits:

Pimiento Cheese
Prep a batch of White Lily "Light" Biscuits, adding ¼ cup drained chopped pimientos and 1 cup shredded Cheddar cheese along with the milk. Bake as directed, and serve warm, slathered with hot pepper jelly.

Lemon Basil
Prep a batch of White Lily "Light" Biscuits, adding 1 tablespoon lemon zest and 1 tablespoon finely chopped fresh basil along with the milk. Bake as directed, and serve warm with butter and marmalade.

Mustard and Chive
Prep a batch of White Lily "Light" Biscuits, adding ¼ cup chopped fresh chives and 2 tablespoons whole-grain mustard along with the milk. Bake as directed, and serve warm with sliced country ham and honey.

Blueberry and Honey
Prep a batch of White Lily "Light" Biscuits, adding ¼ cup fresh blueberries and 2 tablespoons runny honey along with the milk. Sprinkle the tops of the biscuits with raw sugar before baking as directed. Serve warm, slathered with butter and even more honey.

Bacon Ranch
Prep a batch of White Lily "Light" Biscuits, adding ¼ cup chopped cooked bacon and 1 tablespoon ranch seasoning mix along with the milk. Bake as directed, and serve warm alongside eggs.

White Lily "Light" Biscuits
Makes about 12

The Southern custom of sopping biscuits in molasses or honey includes placing half of a biscuit, buttered side down, in the molasses and pushing it around with a fork before taking a bite. Historically, sopping the biscuit with your hands was considered bad manners and a child who did so would be admonished with, "Use your fork!"

- 2 cups White Lily Self-Rising Flour
- ¼ teaspoon salt
- ¼ cup cold all-vegetable shortening, unsalted butter, or lard, cubed
- ⅔ cup cold whole milk*

Honey and butter, to serve

1. Preheat oven to 500°.
2. In a large bowl, stir together flour and salt. Using a pastry blender or 2 forks, cut in cold shortening, butter, or lard until it is pea-size. Gradually add cold milk, stirring just until dry ingredients are moistened.
3. Turn out dough onto a lightly floured surface. Knead gently 2 to 3 times. Gently pat or roll dough to ½-inch thickness. Using a 2-inch round cutter dipped in flour, cut dough without twisting cutter, leaving as little dough between cuts as possible, rerolling scraps once. Place, with sides touching, on a baking sheet.
4. Bake until tops are golden brown, 8 to 10 minutes. Serve hot.

You can substitute the milk with ¾ cup cold whole buttermilk.

Biscuits made easy!

1. Use a pastry cutter or 2 forks to cut in the cold shortening, butter, or lard. It is best not to use your hands; the warmth from your hands will cause the fat to soften and melt.
2. The largest pieces of fat left should be pea-size. If the fat is too large, it will leak out of the biscuits and cause the bottoms to burn. If it is too small, the biscuits will not rise as tall and will not have as many layers.
3. Do not overmix the dough. It will result in dense (or tough) biscuits. Knead just until the flour is incorporated. Be sure to re-flour your surface before rolling out the dough. Patting or rolling the dough both work well. Rolling the dough will create a smoother top.
4. When cutting the biscuits, do not twist the cutter. This seals the edges of the biscuit, keeping your biscuits from rising high. Baking with sides touching helps the biscuits to rise higher and have a softer texture after baking. If you like a biscuit with crispy edges, place 1 inch apart on the baking sheet.

Garlic Cheese Biscuits

Makes 20

Is there truly a better combination than garlic and cheese? It is impossible to eat just one of these crowd-pleasers.

2½ cups White Lily Self-Rising Flour
¼ cup cold vegetable shortening, cubed
1 cup shredded Cheddar cheese*
1 cup cold whole milk
½ cup salted butter or margarine, softened
1 tablespoon fresh chopped parsley (optional)
1 teaspoon garlic powder

1. Position oven rack in top third of oven. Preheat oven to 450°.

2. In a large bowl, place flour. Using a pastry blender or 2 forks, cut in cold shortening until shortening is pea-size. Gradually stir in cheese and cold milk until flour is moistened and dough holds together. Drop dough by rounded, heaping tablespoonfuls onto a lined baking sheet 1 inch apart.

3. Bake until tops are lightly golden, 9 to 11 minutes, rotating pan halfway through baking.

4. In a small bowl, stir together butter or margarine, parsley (if using), and garlic powder, and brush onto hot biscuits. Serve hot. Refrigerate any leftover garlic butter.

Use any flavor of shredded cheese you desire. When measuring the cheese, 1 cup equals 4 ounces.

Kitchen Tip

If a recipe calls for self-rising flour and you have only all-purpose flour on hand, use this simple formula: for 1 cup While Lily Self-Rising Flour, substitute 1 cup While Lily All-Purpose Flour, 1½ teaspoons baking powder, and ½ teaspoon salt.

Flaky Layer Buttermilk Biscuits

Makes about 12

Brian Hart Hoffman, editor of Bake from Scratch *magazine, developed these biscuits to honor his love of White Lily Flour.*

3½   cups White Lily All-Purpose Flour
2   tablespoons granulated sugar
1   tablespoon baking powder
1½   teaspoons salt
½   teaspoon baking soda
1¼   cups cold unsalted butter, cubed
1   cup cold whole buttermilk
1   large egg, lightly beaten
Flaked sea salt, for sprinkling
Softened butter and honey, to serve

1. Preheat oven to 425°. Line a baking sheet with parchment paper.

2. In a large bowl, whisk together flour, sugar, baking powder, salt, and baking soda. Using a pastry blender or 2 forks, cut in cold butter until mixture is crumbly and butter pieces are smaller than a pea. Stir in cold buttermilk until a shaggy dough forms.

3. Turn out dough onto a lightly floured surface. Pat dough into a rectangle, and cut into fourths. Stack each fourth on top of each other, and pat into a rectangle. Repeat procedure 3 times. Pat or roll dough to 1-inch thickness. Using a 2½-inch round cutter dipped in flour, cut dough without twisting cutter, rerolling scraps as necessary. Place 2 inches apart on prepared pan. Freeze until cold, about 10 minutes.

4. Brush dough with egg, and sprinkle with sea salt.

5. Bake until golden brown, about 15 minutes. Serve warm with softened butter and honey.

Scones

Makes 6

Whether you serve them up with coffee as a special breakfast or with tea for an afternoon pick-me-up, scones are the perfect vessel for your favorite spreads and jams.

2¼ cups White Lily All-Purpose Flour
¼ cup granulated sugar
1½ teaspoons baking powder
¼ teaspoon baking soda
¼ teaspoon salt
¼ cup cold unsalted butter or margarine, cubed
⅔ cup cold whole buttermilk
2 large eggs, divided
Jam and butter, to serve

1. Preheat oven to 400°.

2. In a large bowl, stir together flour, sugar, baking powder, baking soda, and salt. Using a pastry blender or 2 forks, cut in cold butter or margarine until it is pea-size.

3. In a small bowl, whisk together cold buttermilk and 1 egg. Gradually stir into flour mixture.

4. Turn out dough onto a lightly floured surface, and knead gently 2 to 3 times. Gently pat or roll dough into a ¾-inch-thick circle. Freeze for 10 minutes.

5. Using a knife dipped in flour, cut dough circle into 6 wedges, and place ½ inch apart on a baking sheet.

6. In a small bowl, lightly whisk remaining 1 egg, and brush egg on top of dough.

7. Bake until lightly browned, 15 to 20 minutes. Serve warm or at room temperature with jam and butter.

Kitchen Tip

For a fun variation, add ½ cup raisins or dried cranberries to dough, and bake as directed. In a small bowl, combine ¼ cup confectioners' sugar, 1 tablespoon whole milk or heavy whipping cream, and ⅔ teaspoon orange extract. Drizzle glaze on top of warm scones.

Cathead Biscuits

Makes about 8

About as "big as a cat's head," these classics were born out of a need to make biscuits quickly, but they remain a favorite for their light and tender texture.

5   cups White Lily Self-Rising Flour
10   tablespoons cold unsalted butter or all-vegetable shortening, cubed
1½   cups plus 2 tablespoons cold whole buttermilk, divided
Salted butter, melted

1. Preheat oven to 425°. Line a baking sheet with parchment paper.

2. In a large bowl, place flour. Using a pastry blender or 2 forks, cut in cold butter or shortening until it is pea-size. Gradually add 1½ cups cold buttermilk, stirring just until flour is moistened; add up to remaining 2 tablespoons cold buttermilk, 1 tablespoon at a time, if necessary.

3. Turn out dough onto a lightly floured surface. Knead gently 2 to 3 times. Gently pat or roll dough to 1-inch thickness. Using a 3-inch round cutter dipped in flour, cut dough without twisting cutter, leaving as little dough between cuts as possible, rerolling scraps once. Place, with sides touching, on prepared pan.

4. Bake until tops are golden brown, 15 to 20 minutes. Brush with melted butter; serve hot.

Kitchen Tip

The size of these biscuits makes them ideal for filling with fried chicken, breakfast sausage patties, or fried eggs and bacon.

Peach Cobbler with Biscuit Topping

Makes 6 to 8 servings

When selecting cobbler ingredients, it is best to choose the peaches with the sweetest aroma. If you see peaches that are green in color, they have been harvested too soon and will not ripen.

6   cups sliced peeled fresh peaches (6 to 7 medium peaches), or 2 (16-ounce) packages frozen peach slices, thawed and drained

1¼   cups plus 1 tablespoon granulated sugar, divided

1⅔   cups plus 2 tablespoons White Lily Self-Rising Flour, divided

½   teaspoon ground cinnamon

2   tablespoons unsalted butter, melted and divided

¼   cup cold butter, cubed

⅓ to ½ cup whole milk

Vanilla ice cream, to serve

1. Preheat oven to 450°.

2. In a large saucepan, combine peaches, 1 cup sugar, 2 tablespoons flour, and cinnamon. Heat over medium-high heat until hot and sauce begins to thicken, about 5 minutes.

3. Brush a 9-inch round baking dish or an 11x8-inch baking dish with 1 tablespoon melted butter. Pour peach mixture into pan, and set aside.

4. In a large bowl, combine ¼ cup sugar and remaining 1⅔ cups flour. Using a pastry blender or 2 forks, cut in cold butter until mixture resembles coarse crumbs. Gradually add ⅓ cup milk, stirring just until dry ingredients are moistened and dough holds together; add up to remaining 3 tablespoons milk, 1 tablespoon at a time, if necessary.

5. Turn out dough onto a lightly floured surface. Fold dough in half, and press lightly 2 or 3 times so it can be rolled and will not stick. Roll to about ¼-inch thickness. Using a 2-inch round cutter, cut dough. Press cut dough gently on top of warm peach mixture. Drizzle with remaining 1 tablespoon melted butter, and sprinkle with remaining 1 tablespoon sugar.

6. Bake until biscuits are golden brown, 15 to 20 minutes. Serve warm with ice cream.

Kitchen Tip

For a blueberry cobbler, replace the peaches with 4 cups fresh blueberries or 2 (16-ounce) packages frozen blueberries, reduce the sugar in the blueberry mixture to ¾ cup, and replace cinnamon with 1 teaspoon fresh lemon juice.

Grandma's Gravy

Makes 5 cups

A weekend treat at Grandma's house for many Southerners, biscuits and gravy are a surefire way to get children out of bed and into the kitchen. You can use a different combination of meats to get the base for this gravy, but we prefer the ones here best.

1 (8-ounce) package ground pork sausage
8 slices bacon
⅓ cup White Lily All-Purpose Flour
3½ cups whole milk, room temperature
1¼ teaspoons salt
Biscuits, to serve
Garnish: fresh sage leaves

1. In a large heavy-bottomed skillet, cook sausage over medium heat until browned and crispy. Remove from skillet using a slotted spoon, and reserve letting drain on paper towels, reserving drippings in skillet. Cook bacon in the same skillet over medium heat until browned and cripsy. Remove from skillet using a slotted spoon, and let drain on paper towels, reserving drippings in skillet.
2. Add flour to skillet, and cook over medium-high heat, stirring constantly, until slightly browned, about 1 minute. Add milk and salt. Cook, stirring constantly, until mixture begins to thicken, 5 to 7 minutes.
3. Stir sausage into gravy. Serve over biscuits with bacon. Garnish with sage, if desired.

BISCUIT TOPPINGS

Flavored butters make special toppings for biscuits, pancakes, and vegetables. Orange Honey Butter is excellent on broccoli or carrots.

Garlic Butter
Makes ½ cup

- ½ cup salted butter, softened
- 1 tablespoon fresh chopped parsley (optional)
- 1 teaspoon garlic powder

1. In a small bowl, stir together butter, parsley (if using), and garlic powder. Refrigerate in an airtight container.

Orange Honey Butter
Makes ½ cup

- ½ cup salted butter, softened
- 2 tablespoons honey
- 2 teaspoons orange zest

1. In a small bowl, stir together all ingredients. Cover and refrigerate until ready to use.

Cinnamon Molasses Butter
Makes ½ cup

- ½ cup salted butter, softened
- 1 tablespoon molasses
- ½ teaspoon ground cinnamon

1. In a small bowl, stir together all ingredients. Refrigerate in an airtight container.

CHAPTER 2

CORNBREAD

If you're looking for the perfect addition to
a quick dinner for two or a simple way to add bulk to
a family meal, a hot skillet of fresh cornbread is
easy and delicious every time.

CORNBREAD TIPS

The most important secrets to good cornbread? Mix it with a light hand and cook it in a hot pan. Here are some other tips to help you cook your cornbread just right:

◆ Use whole-kernel cornmeal. The whole kernel contains natural corn oil, and it makes your bread taste like fresh sweet corn. Many mills remove the bran and germ, which removes the flavorful parts of the corn and leaves basically corn flour. White Lily packs coarsely ground, whole-kernel cornmeal into every bag and blends it with the ingredients you need for making perfect, full-flavored cornbread every time.

◆ Measure cornmeal the same way you measure flour.

◆ Mix your cornmeal batter until all the ingredients are moist—the batter will not be smooth. Avoid overmixing or your cornbread will be tough and have tunnels and peaked tops.

◆ Preheat your skillet in the oven for crispy cornbread edges. Use a cast-iron skillet and pour in a little corn oil or bacon grease. The skillet will sizzle when the cornbread batter is added, and your cornbread will have a crisp, browned crust.

CAST IRON BASICS

We season for a reason!

When it comes to cooking cornbread, it is well worth the effort to season a cast-iron skillet. Cornbread cooked in cast iron has a crispy, crunchy outside and a moist, buttery inside. Here are some tips on how to get the most out of your cast-iron skillet:

◆ Wash your new skillet with soap and water. This will be the only time you do this.

◆ Dry the skillet, and rub the surface with a paper towel dipped in shortening or vegetable oil.

◆ Put your skillet in a 250° oven for several hours. The oil will turn dark brown. Your skillet is now ready for cooking, but the flavor will continue to improve with time.

◆ Care for your seasoned skillet by simply wiping it off with a damp or dry cloth. Washing it with soap and water will undo the seasoning of the skillet. Dry well, and re-coat with oil between uses.

◆ Pour a little oil in the skillet each time you cook. This will keep food from sticking to the skillet.

White Lily Southern Cornbread

Makes 1 (8-inch) skillet

Should cornbread be sweet? Since this great debate is ongoing among Southern cuisine lovers, we've made the sugar in our recipe optional so you can adjust the flavor to your personal preference. Want the best of both worlds? Spread honey or molasses on your unsweetened cornbread.

1¼   **cups whole milk or whole buttermilk***
¼   **cup vegetable oil**
1   **large egg, lightly beaten**
2   **cups White Lily Self-Rising Cornmeal Mix**
1 to 2 tablespoons granulated sugar (optional)

1. Preheat oven to 425°. Butter an 8-inch cast-iron skillet or an 8-inch square baking pan. Place skillet in oven to preheat, about 8 minutes.
2. In a large bowl, stir together milk or buttermilk, oil, and egg. Add cornmeal mix and sugar (if using), stirring just until moistened. (Batter should be lumpy.) Pour batter into prepared skillet or pan.
3. Bake until golden brown, 25 to 27 minutes. Serve hot.

*Use 1½ cups if using whole buttermilk.

Kitchen Tips

For cornbread muffins, fill 16 buttered muffin cups two-thirds full, and bake at 425° for 20 to 25 minutes. For corn sticks, preheat well-buttered heavy corn stick pans (16 to 18 wells total). Fill almost full. Bake at 425° for 12 to 16 minutes.

Cornmeal-Breaded Catfish and Hush Puppies

Makes 4 servings

Have you noticed that catfish are jumping onto menus everywhere? That's because catfish were largely ignored until farm raising began. The farm-raised fish are grain-fed, and the result is a better, more mellow taste. Including hush puppies at your fish fry is also encouraged!

Vegetable oil, for frying
4   (8- to 10-ounce) catfish fillets
½   teaspoon ground black pepper
1½ cups White Lily Self-Rising Cornmeal Mix
Lemon slices, to serve

1. In a large Dutch oven, pour oil to a depth of 2½ inches, and heat over medium heat until a deep-fry thermometer registers 375°.
2. Fill a large bowl with ice water. Add catfish, and submerge for 2 minutes. (This helps breading adhere to fish.) Remove catfish, and sprinkle all over with pepper.
3. In a shallow dish, place cornmeal mix. Dredge catfish in cornmeal, gently pressing to adhere.
4. Fry catfish in batches until golden brown, about 4 minutes per side. Remove from pot, and let drain on paper towels. (If desired, keep catfish warm by placing them on a baking sheet in a 200° oven until ready to serve.) Serve with lemon slices.

Hush Puppies

Makes about 28

Legend has it that this name comes from tossing bits of fried fish breading to the dogs to get them to hush their howling. That may not be true, but it is a fact that it isn't a fish fry without hush puppies alongside.

Vegetable oil, for frying
1½ cups White Lily Self-Rising Cornmeal Mix
⅔   cup whole milk
1   large egg, lightly beaten
¼   cup finely chopped white onion

1. In a deep saucepan or Dutch oven, pour oil to a depth of 2½ inches, and heat over medium heat until a deep-fry thermometer registers 375°.
2. In a large bowl, stir together cornmeal mix, milk, and egg just until combined. Stir in onion.
3. Drop batter by rounded tablespoonsfuls, a few at a time, into hot oil. Fry until golden brown, about 1 minute per side. Let drain on paper towels.

Kitchen Tip

For Cajun hush puppies, add in ½ teaspoon ground red pepper, ½ teaspoon dried thyme leaves, ¼ teaspoon ground white pepper, ¼ teaspoon ground black pepper, ⅛ teaspoon dried oregano leaves, and 1 minced garlic clove with cornmeal mix. Substitute white onion with green onion. Prepare and cook as directed.

Cornbread-Sausage Dressing

Makes 10 to 12 servings

Dressing made with cornbread is a Southern favorite, and most won't realize that sausage is included in this dish. This recipe stretches far and can feed the whole family or stuff the Thanksgiving turkey.

1 tablespoon unsalted butter, divided
1 (2-pound) bag White Lily Self-Rising Cornmeal Mix
2½ cups whole milk
⅓ cup vegetable oil
4 large eggs, divided and lightly beaten
1 pound ground pork sausage
1 cup chopped yellow onion
2 cups chopped celery
2 (10.5-ounce) cans cream of chicken soup
2½ cups chicken broth
1 cup hot water
1 tablespoon ground sage
1 teaspoon poultry seasoning
½ teaspoon salt
½ teaspoon ground black pepper
Garnish: fresh celery leaves

1. Preheat oven to 425°. Lightly butter a 13x9-inch baking dish.

2. In a large bowl, stir together cornmeal mix, milk, oil, and 2 eggs until well combined. Pour into prepared pan.

3. Bake until golden brown, about 30 minutes. Let cool completely in pan. Remove from pan, and wipe pan clean. Reduce oven temperature to 400°. Using remaining ½ tablespoon butter, lightly butter pan.

4. In a large skillet, cook sausage, onion, and celery over medium heat, stirring frequently, until sausage is browned and crumbly and vegetables are tender, 10 to 15 minutes.

5. In a very large bowl, crumble cornbread. Add sausage mixture. Stir in soup, broth, 1 cup hot water, sage, poultry seasoning, salt, pepper, and remaining 2 eggs. Spoon into prepared pan.

6. Bake until golden brown, 40 to 45 minutes. Let cool for 10 minutes. Garnish with fresh celery leaves, if desired. Serve warm.

Kitchen Tip

The dressing can be made ahead of time. Proceed with recipe as directed through step 5; cover and refrigerate overnight. Let stand at room temperature for at least 30 minutes before baking. Cover and bake for at least 15 minutes; uncover and bake until golden brown, 40 to 45 minutes more.

Southwestern-Style Cornbread

Makes 1 (10-inch) skillet

Once you've perfected your classic cornbread recipe, you might be ready to amp things up. This zesty version adds an extra punch of fun and flavor you'll go back to again and again.

2 cups White Lily Self-Rising Cornmeal Mix
1 (14.75-ounce) can cream-style corn
1 (8-ounce) container sour cream
1 to 2 jalapeños, seeded and finely chopped
¼ cup vegetable oil
2 large eggs, lightly beaten
3 tablespoons finely chopped red bell pepper
½ cup shredded Monterey Jack cheese with peppers

1. Preheat oven to 350°. Butter a 10-inch cast-iron skillet. Place skillet in oven to preheat.
2. In a large bowl, stir together cornmeal mix, corn, sour cream, jalapeño, oil, eggs, and bell pepper just until moistened. Carefully pour half of batter into hot skillet; sprinkle evenly with cheese. Pour remaining batter on top of cheese.
3. Bake until edges begin to pull away from skillet and top is lightly golden, about 45 minutes. Let cool for 10 minutes before serving.

Kitchen Tip

Leaving the seeds in the jalapeño adds more heat to the cornbread. Wear thin plastic gloves when chopping hot peppers.

Cornmeal Pancakes

Makes about 16

Perfect to wake up to in the morning or cozy up with at suppertime, these cornmeal pancakes are also perfect served with thin, grilled pork chops for a quick, comforting meal after a busy day.

2 cups White Lily Self-Rising Cornmeal Mix
2 cups whole buttermilk (see kitchen tip), room temperature
2 large eggs, lightly beaten
2 tablespoons unsalted butter, melted
Butter or margarine, fresh fruit, and syrup, to serve

1. Lightly butter a griddle. Heat griddle to 400°.
2. In a large bowl, stir together cornmeal mix, buttermilk, eggs, and melted butter just until moistened. (Batter will be slightly lumpy.)
3. Drop batter by ¼ cupfuls onto griddle. Cook until golden brown, about 1 minute per side. Serve with butter or margarine, fruit, and syrup.

Kitchen Tip

For thinner pancakes, increase the amount of buttermilk used; for thicker pancakes, descrease the amount of buttermilk used.

Creamy Corn Spoon Bread

Makes 6 servings

Spoon bread is a cross between grits and a soufflé. Using self-rising cornmeal makes this an easy dish to prepare.

1 cup White Lily Self-Rising Cornmeal Mix
1½ cups whole milk
1 cup cream-style corn
¼ cup unsalted butter or margarine, softened
3 large eggs, separated
1 tablespoon granulated sugar
Butter, to serve
Garnish: chopped green onion

1. Preheat oven to 325°. Butter a 2-quart baking dish.
2. In large saucepan, combine cornmeal mix and milk. Cook over medium-high heat, stirring constantly, until mixture is very thick. Remove from heat, and stir in corn, butter or margarine, egg yolks, and sugar.
3. In a medium bowl, beat egg whites with a mixer at high speed until stiff peaks form. Carefully fold egg whites into batter. Pour into prepared pan.
4. Bake until a knife inserted in center comes out clean, 55 minutes to 1 hour and 5 minutes. Serve immediately with butter. Garnish with green onion, if desired. Spoon bread will settle upon standing.

Kitchen Tip

For the most volume when whipping egg whites, make sure your bowl and beaters are clean.

Homemade Hot Tamales

Makes about 24

Tamales are easy to customize and perfect for freezing.

- 1   pound ground chuck
- 1   medium onion, finely chopped
- 5¼   cups White Lily Self-Rising Cornmeal Mix, divided
- 1 to 2 jalapeños (optional), seeded and finely diced
- 3   tablespoons chili powder, divided
- ½   teaspoon salt
- ½   teaspoon garlic powder
- ½   teaspoon ground black pepper
- ¾   cup plus 2 tablespoons vegetable shortening
- 1¾ to 2½ cups boiling water
- Tamale papers or corn husks
- Fresh Tomato Salsa (recipe follows)
- Lime wedges, to serve
- Garnish: chopped fresh cilantro

1. Soak tamale papers or corn husks in warm water until soft, at least 30 minutes.

2. In a large skillet, cook beef and onion over medium heat until beef is browned. Remove from heat, and stir in ¼ cup cornmeal mix, jalapeños (if using), 2 tablespoons chili powder, salt, garlic powder, and black pepper. Set aside, and let cool.

3. In a large bowl, stir together shortening, remaining 5 cups cornmeal mix, and remaining 1 tablespoon chili powder until well combined. Stir in 1½ to 2 cups boiling water until a soft dough forms. (You may not need all of the water.)

4. Spread 3 tablespoons cornmeal mixture on each paper or husk, making a 4½x3½-inch rectangle. Place 1 tablespoon cooled beef mixture lengthwise down center of rectangle. Fold up bottom edge of paper or husk so cornmeal mixture wraps completely around beef mixture. Continue rolling, and tuck in both sides of paper to produce a smooth, sealed roll. (Tamales may be tied or just folded.)

5. In a large steamer pot, add water to a depth of 1 inch, and bring to a boil over high heat. Reduced heat to medium-low. Carefully place tamales, seam side down, in steamer insert, and place insert into steamer. Cover and cook until tamales are tender and cooked through, about 45 minutes. Drain. Remove papers or husks. (If freezing, leave tamales wrapped.) Serve with Fresh Tomato Salsa and lime wedges. Garnish with cilantro, if desired.

Fresh Tomato Salsa

Makes about 3 cups

- 2   tomatoes, chopped (about 2½ cups)
- 1   jalapeño, chopped and seeded
- ½   cup chopped yellow onion
- 2   tablespoons chopped fresh cilantro
- 2   tablespoons fresh lime juice
- 1   clove garlic, minced
- ¼   teaspoon salt

1. In a medium bowl, stir together all ingredients until combined. Refrigerate until ready to use.

Folding a tamale made easy!

1. Remove tamale papers (or corn husks) from water, letting excess water drip off. Place on countertop or cutting board. Press cornmeal mixture out using your fingertips into a 4½x3½-inch rectangle.

2. Place 1 tablespoon beef mixture lengthwise down the center. You will enclose the beef within the cornmeal mixture, so make sure to leave a border on all sides.

3. When rolling up the tamale, start along one of the long sides of the rectangle. Using the paper to help, fold so the cornmeal mixture meets and fully encloses or wraps around the beef mixture and then continue rolling.

4. Tie the ends after folding to keep the tamale sealed. To create the small strips to tie with, remove a soaked corn husk from the water. Pinch and pull small sections of the paper, and it will naturally tear. Fold one end at a time, and tie with a double knot.

CHAPTER 3

SOUTHERN SUPPER STAPLES

Show off your best Southern cooking skills with these suppertime must-haves—and when you ask, "Y'all want seconds?" the answer will always be, "Yes!"

Chicken and Dumplings with Vegetables

Makes 6 servings

Classic chicken and dumplings was historically popular because—with well-made dumplings—only a few bits of chicken could turn into a full meal. Today, the hearty favorite is just as popular, and we added vegetables to this recipe to make it a well-rounded one-pot dish.

1 (3- to 4-pound) whole chicken, cut into 8 pieces*
8 cups water
1 medium onion, quartered
2 dried bay leaves
4 carrots, peeled, halved lengthwise, and sliced into 1-inch pieces (about 1 cup)
1 medium onion, chopped into 1-inch pieces (about 2½ cups)
2 stalks celery, sliced into 1-inch pieces (about 1 cup)
2 cups White Lily Self-Rising Flour
¼ cup cold all-vegetable shortening, cubed
¾ cup cold whole milk or whole buttermilk**
¼ cup unsalted butter
¼ cup White Lily All-Purpose Flour
¼ cup half-and-half
1 teaspoon salt
½ teaspoon ground black pepper

1. In a Dutch oven or large stockpot, bring chicken, 8 cups water, quartered onion, and bay leaves to a boil over high heat. Reduce heat to low, cover, and cook until an instant-read thermometer inserted in thickest portion of chicken registers 165°, about 30 minutes. Remove chicken, and let cool enough to handle.

Remove meat from bones, cut into 1-inch pieces, and refrigerate until ready to use. Return skin and bones to pot, and cook covered over medium-low heat for up to 4 hours. Strain broth, and reserve in a bowl, discarding skin and bones.

2. Place carrots, chopped onion, and celery in a steamer basket set over simmering water. Cover and steam just until tender, about 10 minutes. Set aside.

3. In a large bowl, place self-rising flour. Using a pastry blender or 2 forks, cut in cold shortening until mixture resembles coarse crumbs. Stir in cold milk or buttermilk until well combined. Turn out dough onto a lightly floured surface, and roll to about ¼-inch thickness. Using a pizza cutter or knife, cut into 2x½-inch strips.

4. In same Dutch oven or stockpot, melt butter over medium-high heat. Whisk in all-purpose flour. Cook, whisking constantly, for 1 minute. Whisk in 4 cups reserved broth. (Freeze any remaining broth for another use.) Add half-and-half, salt, and pepper. Bring to a boil over high heat. Add chicken and vegetable mixture, and return to a boil. Add dumplings; reduce heat to medium-high, cover, and cook until dumplings are firm, about 15 minutes. Serve immediately.

*Make sure chicken pieces are around the same size.
**If using whole buttermilk, use 1 cup.*

⊢ Kitchen Tip ⊢

Vegetable mixture can be prepped ahead of time and refrigerated until ready to use.

Country-Fried Steak with Gravy

Makes 4 servings

Some areas of the country call this beef entrée chicken-fried steak. The meat can either be purchased already tenderized or can be tenderized by pounding. Make sure you chill the steak on ice for 1 minute before breading it to help the crust stay on better.

⅓ cup plus ¼ cup vegetable oil, divided
4½ cups whole milk, divided
3 large eggs
1⅓ cups plus ¼ cup White Lily All-Purpose Flour, divided
2 teaspoons salt, divided
⅛ teaspoon garlic powder
4 cubed beef steaks (¾ to 1 pound total)
¼ teaspoon ground black pepper, plus more to taste
Mashed potatoes, to serve
Garnish: chopped fresh chives

1. In a large heavy-bottomed skillet, heat ⅓ cup oil over medium-high heat until a deep-fry thermometer registers 350°.

2. In a small bowl, whisk together 1 cup milk and eggs. In a medium bowl, stir together 1⅓ cups flour, 1 teaspoon salt, and garlic powder. Dip steaks in milk mixture, letting excess drip off; dredge in flour mixture, shaking off excess.

3. Fry for 5 to 7 minutes per side. Remove from skillet, and let drain on paper towels.

4. Add remaining ¼ cup oil to skillet. Stir in remaining ¼ cup flour until well combined. Add remaining 3½ cups milk, and bring to a boil over medium heat, stirring constantly. Reduce heat to low, and add pepper and remaining 1 teaspoon salt.

5. Return steaks to skillet. Cover and cook over low heat, stirring occasionally, until tender and an instant-read thermometer inserted in thickest portion of steak registers 160°, about 40 minutes. Spoon gravy over steaks before serving. Season with pepper. Serve with mashed potatoes; garnish with chives, if desired.

⊢ *Kitchen Tip* ⊣

If you can't find cube steak, then cover the steak (usually top round or top sirloin) with plastic wrap and pound with the back of a small cast-iron skillet.

Chicken Pot Pie

Makes 6 servings

This recipe includes two easy toppings: a biscuit crust and a piecrust. Choose your favorite for a one-dish meal that includes plenty of vegetables.

4   carrots, peeled and sliced into ½-inch pieces (about 2 cups)
1   medium onion, finely chopped (about 2¼ cups)
3   stalks celery, sliced into ½-inch pieces (about 1½ cups)
¼   cup unsalted butter
7   tablespoons White Lily All-Purpose Flour
3   cups homemade chicken broth or 2 (14.5-ounce) cans unsalted chicken broth
¼   cup heavy whipping cream
1   teaspoon salt
½   teaspoon ground black pepper
1½   cups 2-inch-cubed cooked chicken
1   cup frozen peas
Flaky Piecrust (single crust; recipe on page 101) or White Lily "Light" Biscuits (recipe on page 18)
1   large egg, lightly beaten (if using Flaky Piecrust topping)

1. Place carrots, onion, and celery in a steamer basket set over simmering water. Cover and steam just until tender, about 10 minutes. Remove from steamer, and set aside.

2. Preheat oven to 400°.

3. In a large saucepan, melt butter over medium heat. Stir in flour, and cook for 1 minute. Gradually add broth, cream, salt, and pepper, and cook until thickened, about 15 minutes. Stir in vegetable mixture, chicken, and peas. Pour into an 11x8-inch baking dish.

4. If using Flaky Piecrust, gently roll dough into a 13x10-inch rectangle. Place dough on top of filling, and crimp edges, if desired. Vent top as desired, and brush with beaten egg.

5. Bake until piecrust is golden brown, 40 to 45 minutes.

6. If using White Lily "Light" Biscuits, proceed with biscuits recipe through cutting dough in step 3; place dough on top of filling.

7. Bake until biscuits are lightly browned, about 30 minutes.

Kitchen Tip

To assist in rolling the piecrust topping into a rectangle, roll dough from the center diagonally to the left and right, top and bottom.

Spicy Nashville Fried Chicken

Makes 4 to 6 servings

Spice things up and get ready to meet your new go-to take on classic fried chicken.
We recommend serving this up with plenty of pickles for a crunchy, cool contrast.

Vegetable oil, for frying
1 teaspoon kosher salt
10 chicken tenders (about 2 ounces each)
2 cups whole buttermilk
4 large eggs
2 tablespoons hot sauce
3 cups White Lily Self-Rising Flour
2 tablespoons firmly packed light brown
   sugar
1 teaspoon sweet paprika
1 teaspoon garlic salt
1 teaspoon ground red pepper
1 teaspoon crushed red pepper
Biscuits and pickles, to serve

1. In a 12-inch cast-iron skillet, pour oil to a depth of 1½ inches, and heat over medium heat until a deep-fry thermometer registers 345°.

2. Sprinkle salt all over chicken, and let stand for 10 minutes.

3. In a medium bowl, whisk together buttermilk, eggs, and hot sauce until smooth. In another medium bowl, place flour. Add chicken to buttermilk mixture. Remove 1 piece of chicken at a time from buttermilk, letting excess drip off. Dredge in flour, pressing gently to adhere. Place on a rimmed baking sheet. Repeat with remaining chicken.

4. In a medium heatproof bowl, stir together brown sugar, paprika, garlic salt, and red peppers.

5. Fry chicken, 3 pieces at a time, for 2 to 3 minutes, turning twice. Place chicken on a wire rack over a rimmed baking sheet.

6. Carefully remove 1 cup hot oil, and add to sugar mixture; stir until sugar dissolves. Pour evenly over hot chicken. Serve with biscuits and pickles.

Kitchen Tip

Breading the chicken and then letting it stand for a bit before frying helps the coating adhere better.

Tomato Pie

Makes 1 (9½-inch) deep-dish pie

Have you ever come across the most beautiful, deep-red tomatoes and wondered how you could use them all? Your solution lies within this rich and flavorful deep-dish pie.

3 pounds medium tomatoes, sliced ½ inch thick
1 teaspoon salt, divided
Parmesan Pie Dough (recipe follows)
8 thick-cut bacon slices, diced
⅓ cup chopped yellow onion
2½ teaspoons minced garlic
2 cups shredded Cheddar-Jack cheese blend, divided
⅔ cup mayonnaise
⅔ cup chopped fresh basil
⅓ cup thinly sliced fresh chives
1 large egg
1 tablespoon Dijon mustard
¼ teaspoon ground black pepper
Fresh basil leaves
Chopped fresh chives

1. Place tomato slices on paper towels; sprinkle ½ teaspoon salt all over slices. Let stand for 2 hours, patting dry with paper towels every hour.
2. Preheat oven to 400°.
3. On a lightly floured surface, roll Parmesan Pie Dough into a 16-inch circle (⅛ inch thick). Transfer to a 9½-inch deep-dish glass pie plate. Trim edges to ½ inch past edge of plate, if necessary. Fold edges under, and crimp, if desired. Freeze until firm, about 15 minutes.
4. Top prepared crust with a piece of parchment paper, letting ends extend over edges of plate. Add pie weights.
5. Bake until edges look dry, 18 to 20 minutes. Carefully remove paper and weights. Bake until crust is golden brown and dry, 10 to 15 minutes more. Let cool completely on a wire rack, about 30 minutes. Leave oven on.
6. In a medium skillet, cook bacon over medium-high heat until fat is beginning to render, 4 to 5 minutes. Add onion, and cook until bacon is crisp and onion is translucent, 4 to 5 minutes. Stir in garlic; cook until fragrant, about 1 minute.

Remove bacon mixture using a slotted spoon, and let drain on paper towels. Let cool for 20 minutes.
7. In a large bowl, stir together 1¾ cups cheese, mayonnaise, basil, chives, egg, and mustard until combined. Sprinkle with pepper and remaining ½ teaspoon salt. Fold in bacon mixture.
8. Gently spread one-third of cheese mixture in prepared crust; layer with one-third of tomato slices in a slightly overlapping pattern. Repeat layers twice with remaining cheese mixture and remaining tomato slices. Cover edges of pie with foil.
9. Bake until filling is set, 40 to 45 minutes. Sprinkle with remaining ¼ cup cheese, and bake until cheese is melted, 3 to 5 minutes more. Transfer to a wire rack, and let stand for 1 hour before serving. Sprinkle with basil leaves and chopped chives.

Parmesan Pie Dough

Makes 1 (9½-inch) deep-dish crust

2 cups White Lily All-Purpose Flour
2 ounces Parmigiano-Reggiano cheese, grated
¾ teaspoon salt
⅔ cup cold all-vegetable or butter-flavored shortening or unsalted butter, cubed
7 to 9 tablespoons ice water or cold whole milk

1. In a medium bowl, combine flour, cheese, and salt. Using a pastry blender or 2 forks, cut in cold shortening or butter until mixture resembles coarse crumbs. Sprinkle 1 tablespoon ice water or milk over part of mixture. Toss gently with a fork, and push to side of bowl. Repeat procedure, 1 tablespoon ice water or milk at a time, just until mixture is moistened and you can form it into a ball. (Dough should hold together when picked up and pressed and should not crack.) Wrap tightly with plastic wrap, and refrigerate for 30 minutes or up to overnight.

White Chicken Chili Pot Pie

Makes 5 to 6 servings

Add even more bulk and flavor to white chicken chili with this creamy pot pie.

⅓ cup unsalted butter
9 tablespoons White Lily All-Purpose Flour
3¼ cups chicken broth
1 cup diced yellow onion
⅓ cup heavy whipping cream
1¼ teaspoons salt
1¼ teaspoons onion powder
1¼ teaspoons garlic powder
1¼ teaspoons ground black pepper
1 teaspoon smoked paprika
1 teaspoon ground cumin
¾ teaspoon chili powder
1¼ cups shredded Monterey Jack cheese with peppers
⅔ cup sour cream
2 cups shredded rotisserie chicken (white and dark meat)
2 cups frozen whole-kernel yellow corn, thawed
1 (15-ounce) can navy beans, drained and rinsed
2 (4-ounce) cans diced green chiles
Drop Biscuits (recipe follows)

1. Preheat oven to 400°.
2. In a 12-inch cast-iron skillet, melt butter over medium heat. Stir in flour, and cook for 1 minute. Add stock, diced onion, cream, salt, onion powder, garlic powder, black pepper, paprika, cumin, and chili powder, and cook, stirring constantly, until thickened, 15 to 17 minutes.
3. Add cheese to mixture, stirring until melted. Stir in sour cream until combined. Add chicken, corn, beans, and chiles, and stir until well combined.
4. Using 2 spoons, scoop Drop Biscuit dough, and drop, almost touching, on top of filling.
5. Bake until biscuits are golden brown, a wooden pick inserted in center of a biscuit comes out clean, and filling is bubbly, 45 to 50 minutes, covering with foil to prevent excess browning, if necessary.

Drop Biscuits
Makes about 12

1¼ cups White Lily Self-Rising Flour
2 teaspoons granulated sugar
2 tablespoons cold all-vegetable shortening
¾ cup cold whole milk
½ cup shredded Cheddar cheese

1. In a large bowl, combine flour and sugar. Using a pastry blender or 2 forks, cut in cold shortening until shortening is pea-size. Gradually stir in cold milk and cheese until dry ingredients are moistened and dough holds together.

Kitchen Tip

Chili can be made ahead of time. Just make sure the chili is hot before you add the biscuits so they cook evenly.

Buttermilk-Battered Chicken Tenders

Makes 2 to 4 servings

Chicken hasn't always been affordable. Before World War II, a fried chicken dinner was considered a special Sunday treat. Today, boneless chicken breasts make this Southern favorite quick and easy. We recommend serving with honey mustard and fresh biscuits.

Vegetable oil, for frying
8 to 9 chicken tenders (about 2 ounces each)
1 cup whole buttermilk
1½ cups White Lily All-Purpose Flour
2 teaspoons salt
2 teaspoons ground black pepper
2 large eggs
Biscuits and honey mustard, to serve

1. In a large heavy-bottomed skillet, pour oil to a depth of 1½ inches, and heat over medium heat until a deep-fry thermometer registers 365°.

2. In a small bowl, place buttermilk. In a medium bowl, stir together flour, salt, and pepper. In another small bowl, whisk eggs. Working with 1 piece at a time, dip chicken into buttermilk, letting excess drip off. Dredge in flour mixture, shaking off excess. Dip in eggs, letting excess drip off, and dredge in flour, shaking off excess.

3. Fry chicken in batches until golden brown and an instant-read thermometer inserted in thickest portion registers 165°, 2 to 3 minutes per side. Let drain on paper towels. Serve immediately with biscuits and honey mustard, or place on a baking sheet in a 200° preheated oven until ready to serve.

Barbecue Chicken Cornbread Bake

Makes 4 to 6 servings

Throw all of your favorites together in this all-in-one skillet meal. Round it out by serving with a side salad and you've got a delicious, hearty meal for the family.

1	medium red onion
1	tablespoon unsalted butter
¾	cup chopped mini sweet peppers
2	cups rotisserie or pulled chicken
1	cup barbecue sauce
1	(6-ounce) can tomato paste
½	cup chicken broth
2	cups shredded sharp Cheddar cheese, divided
1¼	cups whole milk
¼	cup vegetable oil
1	large egg, lightly beaten
2	cups White Lily Buttermilk Self-Rising Cornmeal Mix
⅓	cup mini sweet pepper rings

1. Preheat oven to 400°.

2. Slice 2 thin rings from onion. Cut rings in half, and reserve. Dice remaining onion, and measure ⅔ cup.

3. Spray a 10-inch cast-iron skillet with cooking spray. Add butter, and melt over medium heat. Add diced onion and chopped peppers, and cook until tender, 5 to 6 minutes. Add chicken, barbecue sauce, tomato paste, and broth, stirring until well combined. Bring to a boil; reduce heat to low. Sprinkle with 1½ cups cheese.

4. In a medium bowl, combine milk, oil, and egg. Add cornmeal mix, and stir just until moistened. (Batter should be lumpy.) Pour batter over cheese in skillet.

5. Bake until top is set, about 10 minutes. Top with pepper rings and reserved sliced onion, and bake until golden brown and a wooden pick inserted in center comes out clean, 8 to 10 minutes more. Sprinkle with remaining ½ cup cheese, and bake until cheese is melted, 2 to 3 minutes more. Serve hot.

Kitchen Tip

Substitute chicken with pulled pork, chopped smoked brisket, cooked ground beef, or cooked ground turkey, if desired.

Sausage, Egg, and Cheese Biscuit Casserole

Makes 9 servings

Prep this recipe in advance for your next overnight guests. You'll wake them up to the irresistible aromas of biscuits and sausage, and there will be plenty for second helpings.

Double recipe White Lily "Light" Biscuits (recipe on page 18), divided
- 1 tablespoon olive oil
- 1 pound mild regular breakfast sausage
- ¾ cup diced red onion
- ¾ cup diced green bell pepper
- 8 large eggs
- 1 cup half-and-half
- 1 tablespoon Dijon mustard
- ½ teaspoon salt
- ½ teaspoon onion powder
- ½ teaspoon garlic powder
- ½ teaspoon ground black pepper
- 3 cups shredded Colby-Jack cheese blend, divided

1. Position oven rack in center of oven. Preheat oven to 375°.

2. Proceed with White Lily "Light" Biscuits recipe through kneading in step 3. On a lightly floured surface, gently pat or roll half of dough into a 12x8-inch rectangle. Place in bottom of an 11x7-inch baking dish. Cover and refrigerate until ready to use.

3. Gently pat or roll remaining dough to ½-inch thickness. Using a 2-inch round cutter dipped in flour, cut dough into 9 biscuits, rerolling scraps once if necessary. Place on a rimmed baking sheet lined with parchment paper, cover, and refrigerate until ready to use.

4. In a medium skillet, heat oil over medium heat. Add sausage, and cook until browned and crumbly, about 10 minutes. Remove sausage using a slotted spoon, and let drain on paper towels.

5. In same skillet, cook red onion and bell pepper over medium heat, stirring occasionally, just until soft, 3 to 4 minutes. Remove from heat, and transfer to a small bowl.

6. In a medium bowl, whisk together eggs, half-and-half, mustard, salt, onion powder, garlic powder, and black pepper until frothy.

7. Top White Lily "Light" Biscuit dough in baking dish evenly with sausage, onion mixture, and 1½ cups cheese. Pour egg mixture over cheese, distributing evenly. Place cut White Lily "Light" Biscuit dough evenly on top of egg mixture, gently pressing biscuits into egg mixture. Loosely cover with heavy-duty foil.

8. Bake until edges are slightly brown, 45 to 50 minutes. Uncover and sprinkle with remaining 1½ cups cheese. Bake until biscuits are golden brown, cheese is melted, and an instant-read thermometer inserted in filling registers 175° to 182°, 5 to 6 minutes. Let stand for 10 minutes before serving.

Kitchen Tip

Make the biscuits the night before, cover tightly with plastic wrap, and refrigerate so they can be ready to go.

CHAPTER 4

CAKES

Is there anything better than a gorgeous cake gracing
the center of your dinner table? These beauties pack
the perfect punch of sweetness and comfort.

CAKE BAKING & FROSTING

◆ Measuring ingredients correctly is so important. To measure flour, spoon lightly into a measuring cup made for dry ingredients. Level the flour over the top with a spatula. To measure other ingredients, be sure to use liquid-measuring cups and dry measuring cups as needed. Shortening or brown sugar should be packed into the measuring cup before leveling off.

◆ For most cakes in this book, unsalted butter is recommended.

◆ Ingredients for making cakes need to be removed from the refrigerator ahead of time so they aren't cold going into the batter. Place eggs in slightly warm tap water for 30 minutes before using. Butter should be softened but does not need to get to room temperature.

◆ Substitution for buttermilk: Add 1 tablespoon lemon juice to 1 cup whole milk.

Red Velvet Cake

Makes 1 (8- or 9-inch) cake

Said to have been invented at the Waldorf-Astoria Hotel in New York City, red velvet cake has become such a favorite in the South that it's now considered a Southern dessert.

1 cup all-vegetable shortening, softened
2 cups granulated sugar
4 large eggs, room temperature
2½ cups White Lily All-Purpose Flour
½ cup unsweetened cocoa powder
1 teaspoon baking soda
½ teaspoon salt
1 cup whole buttermilk, room temperature
1 ounce red liquid food coloring
1 teaspoon vanilla extract
Cream Cheese Frosting (recipe follows)

1. Preheat oven to 350°. Butter and flour 2 (9-inch) or 3 (8-inch) round cake pans. Line bottom of pans with parchment paper.
2. In the bowl of a stand mixer fitted with the paddle attachment, beat shortening and sugar at medium speed until fluffy, 3 to 4 minutes, stopping to scrape sides of bowl. Add eggs, one at a time, beating well after each addition.
3. In a medium bowl, sift together flour, cocoa, baking soda, and salt. With mixer on low speed, gradually add flour mixture to shortening mixture alternately with buttermilk, beginning and ending with flour mixture, beating just until combined after each addition. Stir in food coloring and vanilla. Pour batter into prepared pans, smoothing tops with an offset spatula.

4. Bake until a wooden pick inserted in center comes out clean, 25 to 30 minutes. Let cool in pans for 10 minutes. Remove from pans, and let cool completely on wire racks.
5. If using 9-inch pans, halve layers horizontally. Spread 1¼ cups Cream Cheese Frosting between layers. Spread remaining frosting on top and sides of cake.

Cream Cheese Frosting

Makes 10 cups

3 (8-ounce) packages cream cheese, softened
1½ cups unsalted butter, softened
3 pounds confectioners' sugar
1 tablespoon vanilla extract

1. In a very large bowl, beat cream cheese and butter with a mixer at medium-low speed until smooth, scaping sides of the bowl as needed. Gradually add confectioners' sugar and vanilla, beating until smooth. (Add more or less confectioners' sugar to reach desired consistency.)

Kitchen Tip

Make the cake layers ahead of time and freeze. When the cake is halfway thawed, it is easier to cut the cake layers in half. Fill and frost the cake while it is still a little frozen so there are fewer crumbs and it's easier to work with.

Chocolate Layer Cake with Chocolate Silk Frosting

Makes 1 (8-, 9-, or 13x9-inch) cake

Quickly become everyone's favorite potluck guest with this unbeatable chocolate cake.

2 cups White Lily All-Purpose Flour
2 cups granulated sugar
¾ cup unsweetened cocoa powder, sifted
1 teaspoon baking soda
½ teaspoon salt
½ cup whole buttermilk, room temperature
¼ cup vegetable oil
2 large eggs, room temperature
2 teaspoons vanilla extract
1 cup boiling water
Chocolate Silk Frosting (recipe follows)
Garnish: chopped chocolate

1. Preheat oven to 350°. Butter and flour 3 (8-inch) or 2 (9-inch) round cake pans or a 13x9-inch baking pan. If using round cake pans, line bottom of pans with parchment paper.
2. In a large bowl, whisk together flour, sugar, cocoa, baking soda, and salt. Add buttermilk, oil, eggs, and vanilla. Beat with a mixer at medium speed for 2 minutes. Stir in 1 cup boiling water until combined. (Batter will be thin.) Pour batter into prepared pan or pans.
3. Bake until a wooden pick inserted in center comes out clean, 30 to 35 minutes. If using round cake pans, let cool in pans on wire racks for 5 minutes; remove from pans, and let cool completely on wire racks. If using a 13x9-inch cake pan, let cool completely in pan on a wire rack.

4. If using round cake pans, spread Chocolate Silk Frosting between cooled cake layers and on top and sides of cake. If using a 13x9-inch pan, spread Chocolate Silk Frosting on top of cooled cake. Garnish with chopped chocolate, if desired.

Chocolate Silk Frosting
Makes 7 cups

1 cup unsalted butter, softened
5 cups confectioners' sugar
¾ cup unsweetened cocoa powder, sifted
¾ cup heavy whipping cream
2 teaspoons vanilla extract

1. In a large bowl, beat butter with a mixer at medium speed until creamy. Add confectioners' sugar, cocoa, and cream, and beat at low speed until combined. Add vanilla, and beat until smooth and creamy.

The White Lily Cake

Makes 1 (8-, 9-, or 13x9-inch) cake

Our crowning glory in the world of confections, let this beauty grace the center of your table for gatherings large and small.

2½ cups White Lily All-Purpose Flour
1½ cups granulated sugar
1 teaspoon baking powder
1 teaspoon salt
½ teaspoon baking soda
1 cup whole buttermilk, room temperature
¾ cup all-vegetable shortening, cubed
4 large egg whites
2 teaspoons vanilla extract*
White Buttercream Frosting (recipe follows)

1. Preheat oven to 350°. Butter and flour 3 (8-inch) or 2 (9-inch) round cake pans or a 13x9-inch baking pan. If using round cake pans, line bottom of pans with parchment paper.
2. In the bowl of a stand mixer fitted with the whisk attachment, beat flour, sugar, baking powder, salt, and baking soda at low speed until combined. Add buttermilk and shortening, and beat at medium-low speed for 2 minutes, stopping to scrape sides of bowl. Add egg whites and vanilla, and beat for 2 minutes, stopping to scrape sides of bowl. Spread batter into prepared pan or pans. Tap pan or pans on a kitchen towel-lined counter several times to release any air bubbles.
3. Bake until a wooden pick inserted in center comes out clean, 20 to 25 minutes. If using round cake pans, let cool in pans on wire racks for 10 minutes; remove from pans, and let cool completely on wire racks. If using a 13x9-inch cake pan, let cool completely in pan on a wire rack.

4. If using round cake pans, spread White Buttercream Frosting between cooled cake layers and on top and sides of cake. If using a 13x9-inch pan, spread White Buttercream Frosting on top of cooled cake.

For a flavor twist, substitute 1 teaspoon vanilla extract with 1 teaspoon almond, lemon, or coconut extract.

White Buttercream Frosting

Makes 6 cups

2 pounds confectioners' sugar
2 cups unsalted butter, softened
1 teaspoon vanilla extract
¼ teaspoon salt
½ cup heavy whipping cream

1. In the bowl of a stand mixer fitted with the paddle attachment, beat confectioners' sugar, butter, vanilla, and salt at low speed until well combined, about 3 minutes. Add cream, and beat until smooth, about 3 minutes.

Kitchen Tip

To accurately measure all-vegetable shortening for baking, use shortening baking sticks.

1. Place your first layer in the center of the cake plate or board. Place desired amount of frosting onto the cake layer. (We used about 1 cup.)
2. Smooth flat using an offset spatula. Check that everything is level before moving on, or your cake will be crooked.
3. Repeat frosting and smoothing with the other layers.
4. When frosting the top layer, the frosting should extend past the edges of the cake and have a slight overhang. Make sure the top is level. Frosting can be spread smooth, or using the tip of your spatula, add texture to the frosting.
5. Spread remaining frosting on the sides of the cake. For a textured look, use the tip of your spatula.
6. For a smooth look, place a bowl or bench (metal) scraper on the cake stand so the edge of the scraper is vertical. Slowly turn the stand without moving the scraper until the cake is completely covered and the sides are smooth and straight, removing excess frosting from the edge of the scraper as necessary.
7. The slight overhang of frosting from the top of the cake gets pushed up along the edge of the cake after frosting the sides. This is used to create finished edges on the top of the cake. To finish a smooth cake, hold your spatula at a 45-degree angle, starting from the outer edge of the top and bringing it into the center, catching just the extra frosting and smoothing it flat. This will create level and clean the edges. Work in small sections around the cake until complete.

Angel Food Cake

Makes 1 (10-inch) cake

Angel food cakes appeared in the original 1900s White Lily Cookbook. They are best when fresh strawberries are in season.

1⅓ cups sifted White Lily All-Purpose Flour
1¾ cups granulated sugar, divided
1¾ cups egg whites (12 to 14 large egg whites), room temperature
1 teaspoon cream of tartar
¼ teaspoon salt
2 teaspoons vanilla or almond extract
Strawberry Glaze (recipe follows)
Sweetened Whipped Cream (recipe follows)

1. Position oven rack in bottom third of oven. Preheat oven to 350°.
2. In a medium bowl, sift together flour and 1 cup sugar.
3. In a large bowl, beat egg whites, cream of tartar, and salt with a mixer at medium-high speed until foamy. Gradually add remaining ¾ cup sugar, beating until soft peaks form. Add vanilla or almond extract, and beat just until combined. Using a balloon whisk, gently fold in flour mixture in four additions. Spoon batter into an ungreased 10-inch tube pan. Gently run a knife through batter to release any air bubbles.
4. Bake until cake springs back when lightly pressed with a finger, 30 to 35 minutes. Immediately invert pan (onto a bottle if needed), and let cool completely.
5. Using an offset spatula, loosen cooled cake from sides and bottom of pan. Invert cake onto a cake plate. Serve with Strawberry Glaze and Sweetened Whipped Cream.

Strawberry Glaze

Makes 1¾ cups

1 cup water
1 cup sliced fresh strawberries
⅓ cup granulated sugar
1 teaspoon cornstarch
½ chopped fresh strawberries
¼ teaspoon vanilla extract

1. In a medium heavy-bottomed saucepan, bring 4 cups water and strawberries to a boil over medium-high heat; cook for 5 minutes. Transfer to the container of a blender, and process until smooth. Strain through a fine-mesh sieve into same saucepan, discarding solids. Stir in sugar and cornstarch, and bring to a boil over medium heat, stirring constantly; cook for 1 minute. Remove from heat, and stir in chopped strawberries and vanilla. Let cool completely. Cover and refrigerate until ready to serve.

Sweetened Whipped Cream

Makes 1½ cups

¾ cup heavy whipping cream, cold
2 tablespoons confectioners' sugar
½ teaspoon vanilla extract

1. In a medium bowl, beat all ingredients with a mixer at medium speed until soft peaks form. Use immediately.

How to make a soft batter for a light-as-a-feather cake!

1. Add cream of tartar and salt to room temperature egg whites (be sure no yolk has gotten in the whites).
2. Beat egg white mixture at medium-high speed until foamy. Once bubbles have started to form, add sugar in a slow, steady stream. (This can take 1 to 2 minutes.)
3. For angel food cake, whisk the egg white mixture to form soft peaks when the whisk is lifted up.
4. Sift the dry ingredients to remove lumps and evenly distribute the ingredients. Use a whisk to fold in flour to lessen the risk of deflating the egg white mixture.

Brown Sugar Cinnamon Coffee Cake

Makes 1 (8- or 9-inch) cake

Packed with comforting smells and addicting flavors, treat yourself to a big slice of this coffee cake for a relaxing Sunday morning meal or an anytime snack.

½	cup unsalted butter, melted
⅔	cup firmly packed light brown sugar
¼	cup granulated sugar
2	large eggs, room temperature
2	teaspoons vanilla extract
1½	cups White Lily All-Purpose Flour
1½	teaspoons baking powder
¼	teaspoon salt
¾	cup whole milk plain yogurt, room temperature

Pecan Streusel (recipe follows)
Yogurt Glaze (recipe follows)

1. Preheat oven to 350°. Spray an 8- or 9-inch square baking pan with baking spray with flour.
2. In a medium bowl, place melted butter. Whisk in sugars, eggs, and vanilla.
3. In another medium bowl, whisk together flour, baking powder, and salt. Whisk flour mixture into butter mixture. Add yogurt, whisking just until combined. Pour into prepared pan, smoothing top with an offset spatula. Sprinkle with Pecan Streusel.
4. Bake until a wooden pick inserted in center comes out clean, 30 to 40 minutes. Let cool in pan for 15 minutes. Remove from pan, and drizzle with Yogurt Glaze.

Pecan Streusel
Makes about 1½ cups

½	cup White Lily All-Purpose Flour
¼	cup firmly packed light brown sugar
1	teaspoon ground cinnamon
¼	teaspoon salt
½	cup finely chopped pecans
3	tablespoons unsalted butter, melted

1. In a medium bowl, stir together flour, brown sugar, cinnamon, and salt. Stir in pecans. Stir in melted butter until mixture is crumbly. Crumble with your fingertips until desired consistency is reached.

Yogurt Glaze
Makes about 1 cup

1½	cups confectioners' sugar
2	tablespoons whole milk plain yogurt
1	tablespoon whole milk
½	teaspoon vanilla extract

1. In a small bowl, whisk together all ingredients until smooth.

Kitchen Tip

Try substituting almonds or walnuts for the pecans in this recipe for a fun flavor twist.

Southern Caramel Cake

Makes 1 (8-inch) cake

Caramel is a crowd-favorite for a reason. Sweet and smooth, the frosting pairs perfectly with the fluffy cake to create perfect bites every time.

¾   cup unsalted butter, softened
1½   cups granulated sugar
3   large eggs, room temperature
2   teaspoons vanilla extract
1¾   cups White Lily All-Purpose Flour
2   teaspoons baking powder
½   teaspoon salt
¾   cup whole buttermilk, room temperature
Caramel Frosting (recipe follows)

1. Preheat oven to 325°. Butter and flour 2 (8-inch) round cake pans. Line bottom of pans with parchment paper.
2. In the bowl of a stand mixer fitted with the paddle attachment, beat butter and sugar at medium speed until fluffy, 3 to 4 minutes. Add eggs, one at a time, beating well after each addition. Beat in vanilla.
3. In a medium bowl, whisk together flour, baking powder, and salt. With mixer on low speed, gradually add flour mixture to butter mixture alternately with buttermilk, beginning and ending with flour mixture, beating just until combined after each addition. Divide batter between prepared pans, smoothing tops.
4. Bake until lightly golden and a wooden pick inserted in center comes out clean, 30 to 35 minutes. Let cool in pans for 10 minutes. Remove from pans, and let cool completely on wire racks.
5. Spread Caramel Frosting between cooled layers and on top and sides of cake.

Caramel Frosting

Makes 3½ cups

2   cups granulated sugar
¼   cup water
2   tablespoons light corn syrup
½   cup cold unsalted butter, cubed
1   cup warm heavy whipping cream (105° to 110°)
1   cup unsalted butter, softened
2   teaspoons vanilla extract
¼   teaspoon salt
6   cups confectioners' sugar

1. In a large heavy-bottomed saucepan, place granulated sugar.
2. In a small bowl, whisk together ¼ cup water and corn syrup. Pour over granulated sugar, stirring just until sugar is moistened. Cook, without stirring, over medium-high heat until mixture is golden brown. (Brush any sugar crystals on sides of pan with a pastry brush dipped in water.) Remove from heat.
3. Using a long-handled wooden spoon, stir cold butter into sugar mixture until melted. (Mixture will foam.) Slowly add warm cream, stirring until smooth. (If mixture does not get smooth, cook over low heat, stirring until smooth.) Set aside, and let cool until slightly warm, about 1 hour, stirring occasionally.
4. Pour caramel into a large bowl; add softened butter. Beat with a mixer at medium speed until smooth. Add vanilla and salt. With mixer on low speed, gradually add confectioners' sugar, beating just until smooth. Place a sheet of plastic wrap on surface of frosting. Let stand until frosting has reached a spreadable consistency, 20 to 25 minutes.

Pineapple Upside-Down Cake

Makes 1 (10-inch) cake

Southerners can't look twice at a can of pineapple rings without thinking of a fresh pineapple upside-down cake. Break out your cast-iron skillet for this delicious treat.

¼ cup unsalted butter
¾ cup firmly packed light brown sugar
7 canned pineapple rings
7 maraschino cherries
½ cup chopped pecans
½ cup unsalted butter, softened
1 cup granulated sugar
2 large eggs, room temperature
1 teaspoon vanilla extract
2 cups White Lily All-Purpose Flour
2 teaspoons baking powder
½ teaspoon salt
¾ cup whole milk, room temperature

1. Preheat oven to 350°.

2. In a 10-inch cast-iron skillet, place butter; place in oven until butter is melted.

3. Sprinkle brown sugar over butter in skillet. Arrange pineapple rings on top. Place 1 cherry in center of each pineapple ring. Place pecans around pineapple rings in any open spaces.

4. In the bowl of a stand mixer fitted with the paddle attachment, beat softened butter and granulated sugar at medium speed until fluffy, 3 to 4 minutes, stopping to scrape sides of bowl. Add eggs, one at a time, beating well after each addition. Beat in vanilla.

5. In a medium bowl, whisk together flour, baking powder, and salt. With mixer on low speed, gradually add flour mixture to butter mixture alternately with milk, beginning and ending with flour mixture, beating just until combined after each addition. Pour batter over pineapple rings, smoothing top with an offset spatula.

6. Bake until a wooden pick inserted in center comes out clean, 30 to 35 minutes. Let cool in pan for 5 minutes. Run a knife around edges of pan to release sides of cake; carefully invert cake onto a flat serving plate. Serve warm or at room temperature.

⊦ *Kitchen Tip* ⊦

Choose a cast-iron skillet with a helper handle. This will make inverting the cake much easier.

Cream Cheese Pound Cake

Makes 1 (10-inch) cake

Every baker needs a fantastic pound cake recipe in their arsenal, and you just can't go wrong with this cream cheese version.

1½ cups unsalted butter or margarine, softened
1 (8-ounce) package cream cheese, softened
3 cups granulated sugar
6 large eggs, room temperature
1 teaspoon vanilla extract
½ teaspoon almond extract
3 cups White Lily All-Purpose Flour
½ teaspoon salt

1. Preheat oven to 325°. Butter and flour a 10-inch tube pan.

2. In large bowl, beat butter or margarine and cream cheese with a mixer at medium speed until creamy, about 1 minute. Gradually add sugar, beating until fluffy, 2 to 3 minutes, stopping to scrape sides of bowl. Add eggs, one at a time, beating well after each addition. Add in extracts.

3. In another large bowl, whisk together flour and salt. Fold flour mixture into butter mixture just until combined. (Do not overmix.) Spoon batter into prepared pan, and place on a baking sheet.

4. Bake until a wooden pick inserted near center comes out clean, about 1½ hours. Let cool in pan on a wire rack for 10 minutes. Remove from pan, and let cool completely on a wire rack.

Kitchen Tip

This recipe can be made using a hand mixer or a stand mixer.

CHAPTER 5

PIES & FRUIT DESSERTS

Dense, fruity flavors, sky-high meringue,
and fabulously flaky textures will make these
desserts your new go-tos for potlucks and
afternoon snacks alike.

THE ESSENTIALS

Tips for the perfect piecrust!

Be Cool
Before you start mixing your dough, make sure all your ingredients are cold. Most pastry recipes call for cutting fat—like butter, lard, or shortening—into a flour mixture. You want everything to stay cool enough that the finished pastry is flecked with distinct, unmelted nuggets of fat. Some bakers even use the big holes on a box grater to grate frozen butter or lard into flour.

Drizzle, Don't Pour
When a pastry recipe calls for adding water or other liquids, always add drop by drop and use the minimum called for. (You can always add more if the pastry looks dry, but you can't take it away!) Water helps jump-start gluten formation in dough, and using too much can result in a tough crust.

Use a Light Touch
There are a couple of reasons why it's important not to overwork pastry dough. First, the heat of your hands can melt the fat that helps the dough bake up flaky. Second, stretching the dough aggressively will make gluten production go into high gear, which results in stiff, tough pastry.

Chill Out
Before you roll it out, refrigerate your dough for at least 30 minutes. That period of rest gives the gluten in the dough a chance to relax so it's easier to roll out and it won't shrink too much during baking.

Roll Right
It might be tempting to dust flour all over your countertop in preparation for rolling, but try to use some restraint. Every spoonful that is worked into your dough will make it a little bit tougher. Use just enough to keep the dough from sticking and no more.

Sweat the Details
When making a double-crust pie, don't forget to slice vents into the top—they'll help steam escape during baking and keep the bottom crust from turning soggy. And for a deep-golden crust with nice shine, brush the top of your pies with a wash of beaten egg with a splash of water or heavy whipping cream.

Turn Up the Heat
If you don't bake your pie at a high enough temperature, the crust will not turn out crispy. That's why most recipes recommend starting at 425° or higher before reducing the temperature after about 30 minutes.

Get Steamy
When the cold nuggets of fat hit the heat of the oven, they expand to create pockets of steam. And those pockets are the secret to achieving every pie baker's goal: flakiness!

Offer a Shield
Sometimes, pie fillings and crusts cook at different paces. To make sure your crust doesn't scorch before the bake is finished, use a pie shield—or make one by placing a ring of foil over the edge of the crust during the last few minutes of baking.

Flaky Piecrust

Makes 1 (9-inch) single or double crust

For Single-Crust Pie:
1½ cups White Lily All-Purpose Flour
½ teaspoon salt
½ cup cold all-vegetable shortening, butter-flavored shortening, or unsalted butter, cubed
3 to 6 tablespoons ice water or cold milk*

For Double-Crust Pie:
3 cups White Lily All-Purpose Flour
1 teaspoon salt
1 cup cold all-vegetable shortening, butter-flavored shortening, or unsalted butter, cubed
6 to 12 tablespoons ice water or cold milk*

1. In a medium bowl, combine flour and salt. Using a pastry blender or 2 forks, cut in cold shortening or butter until mixture resembles coarse crumbs. Sprinkle 1 tablespoon ice water or cold milk over part of mixture. Toss gently with a fork, and push to side of bowl. Repeat procedure with remaining ice water or cold milk just until mixture is moistened. (Dough should hold together when picked up and pressed and should not crack.) Shape dough into disks (1 disk for single crust, 2 disks for double crust). Wrap tightly in plastic wrap, and refrigerate for 30 minutes or up to overnight.

*If using shortening for a single crust, use 3 to 4 tablespoons water or milk. For unsalted butter, use 5 to 6 tablespoons water or milk. Double measurments for a double crust.

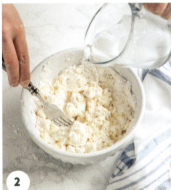

Perfect pie dough made easy!

1. Using a pastry blender to cut in the shortening or butter requires a simple rocking motion until you reach the desired result. If you do not have a pastry blender, you can use 2 forks or your hands. Snap the shortening or butter chunks between your thumb and forefinger, breaking them into smaller pieces until you achieve the correct size. This can warm up your fat, so refrigerate the flour mixture until the fat is cold again, about 15 minutes. Larger butter pieces are needed for pie dough than biscuits. For a super flaky crust, cut in butter until nickel-size. For a slightly less flaky crust, which is nice for a bottom crust because it doesn't absorb as much moisture from fillings, cut in butter until dime-size.
2. Slowly add the liquid to the flour mixture. This allows the dough to come together easier, without heavy kneading.
3. Shape dough into a smooth, even disk. If there are any major cracks in the dough, they cause an uneven edge when rolled. Wrap the dough and refrigerate before rolling. Refrigerating the dough will help the flour hydrate and allow the gluten to relax so it is easier to roll out.

Old-Fashioned Apple Pie

Makes 1 (9-inch) pie

This apple pie recipe is the quintessential American pie. It has been published in a century of White Lily cookbooks.

Flaky Piecrust (recipe on page 101), double crust
- 9 medium Granny Smith or Golden Delicious apples, peeled, cored, and sliced (about 8 cups)
- 1 tablespoon fresh lemon juice
- 1 cup plus 1 tablespoon granulated sugar, divided
- 3 tablespoons White Lily Plain All-Purpose Flour
- ½ teaspoon ground cinnamon
- ⅛ teaspoon ground cloves
- ⅛ teaspoon ground allspice
- ¼ cup cold unsalted butter, cubed
- 1 large egg, lightly beaten

1. Let Flaky Piecrust stand at room temperature for 5 minutes to soften, if necessary. On a very lightly floured surface, using a back-and-forth motion from center, gently roll half of dough into a 12-inch circle, turning dough 45 degrees after each roll and very lightly reflouring work surface as needed to prevent sticking. (Do not roll over edge or it will be thin.) Transfer dough to a 9-inch pie plate, pressing into bottom and up sides. Cover and refrigerate until ready to use.

2. Position oven rack in lower third of oven. Preheat oven to 425°.

3. In a large bowl, toss together apples and lemon juice.

4. In a medium bowl, stir together 1 cup sugar, flour, cinnamon, cloves, and allspice. Add sugar mixture to apple mixture, tossing to coat. Let stand for 15 minutes. Spoon into prepared crust, mounding carefully. Place cold butter on top.

5. On a very lightly floured surface, using a back-and-forth motion from center, gently roll remaining dough into a 12-inch circle, turning dough 45 degrees after each roll and very lightly reflouring work surface as needed to prevent sticking. (Do not roll over edge or it will be thin.) Cut 8 (1½-inch) strips of dough. Arrange dough strips on top of filling in a lattice design, being careful not to stretch dough. Trim edges, fold edges of bottom crust and strips over, and crimp, if desired. Brush with egg, and sprinkle with remaining 1 tablespoon sugar.

6. Bake for 15 minutes. Reduce oven temperature to 375°, and bake until filling is bubbly, about 45 minutes more, loosely covering with foil to prevent excess browning, if necessary. Let cool on a wire rack. Serve warm or at room temperature.

Kitchen Tip

For a ginger-pear pie, substitute apples with Bartlett pears; increase cinnamon to 1 teaspoon; add ¼ teaspoon salt, ¼ teaspoon ground ginger, ¼ teaspoon ground nutmeg, and ¼ teaspoon ground cardamom; and omit cloves and allspice.

1. After rolling the dough out to a 12-inch circle, trim the edges to create a 10-inch circle, and use a ruler to cut dough into strips. These photos show 1½-inch strips of dough.
2. Lay half your strips over the filling, making sure they are equidistant. Rotate pie so strips are horizontal to you.
3. Fold back alternating strips. Place 1 strip perpendicular over horizontal strips.
4. Unfold strips and then fold back the other horizontal strips.
5. Place another strip perpendicular over horizontal strips, making sure to keep everything equidistant.
6. Repeat folding back alternating horizontal strips and placing perpendicular strips 2 more times.
7. Trim strips to be slightly past the bottom crust. Fold ends under and pinch.
8. Fold over edges of bottom crust and strips around the outside edge of the pie plate.
9. To crimp the edges, use one hand's thumb and forefinger on the inside edge of the crust. Use your thumb on the outside edge of the crust to gently press in between your thumb and forefinger.

Blueberry Muffins with Streusel Topping

Makes 12

Blueberries are at the height of their season when the middle of summer sets in the South. These muffins are a sweet offering to overnight guests on a hot Sunday morning. Or for dessert, split the muffins and top with a scoop of ice cream or fruit yogurt.

2 cups plus 2 tablespoons White Lily Self-Rising Flour, divided

⅓ cup plus 2 tablespoons granulated sugar, divided

1 tablespoon unsalted butter, softened

1 teaspoon lemon zest

¼ teaspoon salt

1 cup fresh blueberries, rinsed, drained, and patted dry

¾ cup whole milk

¼ cup vegetable oil

1 large egg, lightly beaten

1. Preheat oven to 400°. Butter bottoms of 12 muffin cups or line with paper liners.

2. In a small bowl, stir together 2 tablespoons flour, 2 tablespoons sugar, and butter until crumbly. Set aside.

3. In a large bowl, stir together lemon zest, salt, remaining 2 cups flour, and remaining ⅓ cup sugar. Transfer ¼ cup mixture to a medium bowl; add blueberries, tossing until combined.

4. In another small bowl, whisk together milk, oil, and egg until combined. Add milk mixture to flour mixture, and stir 5 to 7 times. (Batter will not be completely mixed.) Fold in blueberry mixture. Stir just until ingredients are moistened. (Batter will be lumpy. Do not overmix.) Divide batter among prepared muffin cups, filling two-thirds to three-fourths full. Sprinkle with streusel.

5. Bake until golden brown, 15 to 18 minutes.

Kitchen Tips

For tender muffins, avoid overmixing the batter. Substitute raspberries for blueberries for a flavor option.

Cherry Cobbler

Makes 8 to 10 servings

Need a covered dish to carry to a friend or family gathering? Cherry cobbler is simple, delicious, and easy to scoop and serve to a crowd.

Filling:
- ⅔ cup granulated sugar
- ¼ cup cornstarch
- 2 teaspoons ground cinnamon
- 2 teaspoons lemon zest
- ½ teaspoon salt
- 4 (12-ounce) packages frozen pitted sweet cherries, thawed and drained
- ¼ teaspoon almond extract

Biscuits:
- 1¾ cups White Lily Self-Rising Flour
- 2 tablespoons granulated sugar, divided
- ½ teaspoon salt
- ½ teaspoon lemon zest
- ⅓ cup cold unsalted butter, cubed
- ¾ cup cold whole buttermilk

1. Preheat oven to 400°. Spray a 9-inch deep-dish pie plate with baking spray with flour.

2. For filling: In medium bowl, whisk together sugar, cornstarch, cinnamon, lemon zest, and salt.

3. In a large deep skillet, combine sugar mixture, cherries, and almond extract. Bring to a boil over medium-high heat. Cook, stirring constantly, until slightly thickened, 2 to 3 minutes. Pour mixture into prepared plate.

4. For biscuits: In a large bowl, combine flour, 1 tablespoon sugar, salt, and lemon zest. Using a pastry blender or 2 forks, cut in cold butter until butter is pea-size. Gradually stir in cold buttermilk until dry ingredients are moistened and dough holds together. Drop dough by rounded tablespoonfuls onto filling. Sprinkle with remaining 1 tablespoon sugar.

5. Bake until top of biscuits is golden brown, 20 to 25 minutes. If the biscuits begin to brown too quickly, cover the top loosely with foil.

Peach Hand Pies

Makes about 20

Hand pies turn a classic dessert into an extra-special treat that everyone can grab on the go. A fresh basket of these beauties is also perfect for picnics.

3   cups finely chopped peeled fresh peaches (about 2 large peaches)
¼   cup firmly packed light brown sugar
2   tablespoons unsalted butter, cubed
1   teaspoon fresh lemon juice
¼   teaspoon ground cinnamon
⅛   teaspoon salt
⅛   teaspoon almond extract
1   large egg
1   teaspoon water
Flaky Piecrust (recipe on page 101), double crust
1   tablespoon granulated sugar

1. In a medium saucepan, combine peaches, brown sugar, butter, lemon juice, cinnamon, salt, and almond extract; cook over medium heat until peaches are tender, about 15 minutes. Remove from heat, and let cool completely.

2. Preheat oven to 425°. Line 2 baking sheets with parchment paper.

3. In a small bowl, whisk together egg and 1 teaspoon water.

4. On a lightly floured surface, roll half of Flaky Piecrust to ⅛-inch thickness. Using a 3-inch round cutter, cut dough, rerolling scraps as necessary. Place on prepared pans. Place scant 1 tablespoon peach mixture in center of each round.

5. On a lightly floured surface, roll remaining Flaky Piecrust to ⅛-inch thickness. Using a 3-inch round cutter, cut dough, rerolling scraps as necessary. Brush edges of rounds with egg wash. Place, egg wash side down, on top of filled rounds, crimping edges with a fork dipped in flour. Refrigerate or freeze until dough is firm, 10 to 20 minutes.

6. Brush tops with remaining egg wash, and sprinkle with granulated sugar. Using the tip of a sharp paring knife, cut small vents in top of dough to release steam.

7. Bake until golden brown, 20 to 25 minutes. Let cool slightly on a wire rack before serving.

Kitchen Tip

The pies can be made ahead and frozen before baking. Bake from frozen, adding 5 to 8 minutes to the bake time.

Strawberry Shortcakes

Makes 6 servings

Crisp and crumbly, this recipe is the excuse you need to grab an extra basket of fresh strawberries from your local farmers' market.

- 2 cups White Lily Self-Rising Flour
- ½ cup plus 1 tablespoon granulated sugar, divided
- ½ cup cold unsalted butter or margarine, cubed
- ⅓ cup cold half-and-half, plus more for brushing
- 1 large egg, lightly beaten
- 2 cups sliced fresh strawberries
- ½ cup cold heavy whipping cream

1. Preheat oven to 450°.

2. In a large bowl, stir together flour and ¼ cup sugar. Using a pastry blender or 2 forks, cut in cold butter or margarine until it is pea-size.

3. In a small bowl, whisk together cold half-and-half and egg. Add half-and-half mixture to flour mixture, stirring with a fork just until dry ingredients are moistened.

4. Turn out dough onto a lightly floured surface, and gently knead 2 to 3 times. Gently pat or roll to ½-inch thickness. Using a 3¼-inch round cutter dipped in flour, cut dough, leaving as little dough as possible between cuts, rerolling scraps once. Place ½ inch apart on a baking sheet. Refrigerate or freeze until firm, about 10 minutes.

5. Lightly brush top of dough with cold half-and-half.

6. Bake until golden brown, 12 to 15 minutes.

7. In a large bowl, stir together strawberries and ¼ cup sugar. Let sit at least 10 to 15 minutes, stirring occasionally.

8. In another large bowl, beat cold cream and remaining 1 tablespoon sugar with a mixer at medium-high speed until soft peaks form.

9. Split shortcakes in half. Spoon whipped cream mixture on bottom half of shortcakes, and top with strawberry mixture. Cover with top half of shortcakes.

Kitchen Tip

Prepare the strawberries the night before so all the good juices are released. Add almond extract to the berries and some toasted sliced almonds for extra flavor and texture.

Blind-baking made easy!

Lemon Meringue Pie

Makes 1 (9-inch) pie

Show off your meringue skills and serve up thick slices of this tangy favorite to your loved ones.

Flaky Piecrust (recipe on page 101), single crust

- 4 large eggs, separated and room temperature
- 2 cups granulated sugar, divided
- ⅓ cup plus 1½ teaspoons cornstarch, divided
- 1 cup water
- ½ cup whole milk
- ½ cup fresh lemon juice
- ¼ teaspoon salt, divided
- 2 tablespoons unsalted butter, cubed
- 2 tablespoons lemon zest
- ¾ teaspoon distilled white vinegar
- ¼ teaspoon vanilla extract

1. Preheat oven to 400°.

2. On a lightly floured surface, roll Flaky Piecrust into a 12-inch circle (⅛ inch thick). Transfer to a 9-inch pie plate, pressing into bottom and up sides. Trim edges to ½-inch beyond edge of plate, if necessary. Fold edges under, and crimp, if desired. Prick bottom with a fork. Freeze until firm, about 15 minutes.

3. Top prepared crust with a piece of parchment paper, letting ends extend over edges of plate. Add pie weights.

4. Bake until edges look dry, 15 to 20 minutes. Carefully remove paper and weights. Bake until crust is lightly golden brown and dry, 15 to 20 minutes more. Leave oven on.

5. In a medium bowl, slowly whisk together egg yolks, ½ cup sugar, and ⅓ cup cornstarch.

6. In a medium saucepan, stir together 1 cup sugar, 1 cup water, milk, lemon juice, and ⅛ teaspoon salt. Cook over medium heat, stirring occasionally, until steaming. (Do not boil.) Slowly pour hot sugar mixture into egg yolk mixture, whisking constantly. Return mixture to saucepan, and bring to a boil over medium heat, whisking constantly; cook, whisking constantly, for 1 to 2 minutes. Remove from heat. Stir in butter and lemon zest. Immediately pour into prepared crust.

7. In the bowl of a stand mixer fitted with the whisk attachment, beat egg whites and remaining ⅛ teaspoon salt at medium speed until soft peaks form, about 2 minutes. With mixer on medium speed, add remaining ½ cup sugar in a slow, steady stream, beating until combined. Increase mixer speed to high, and beat until glossy stiff peaks form, about 2 minutes, stopping to scrape sides of bowl halfway through beating.

8. In a small bowl, whisk together vinegar, vanilla, and remaining 1½ teaspoons cornstarch. Add to meringue, and beat at high speed until combined, about 30 seconds. Spoon on top of hot pie, making sure to push it all the way to the edges.

9. Bake until meringue is lightly golden, 10 to 15 minutes. Let cool to room temperature. Refrigerate until ready to serve. Serve chilled or at room temperature.

1. Docking the dough with a fork is essential for blind baking. Without the holes, steam builds up under the crust, causing ballooning. Refrigerating the crust before baking is also important. It hardens the butter and keeps the crust from sliding or shrinking as it heats in the oven. Cold butter steams and creates flakiness, whereas warm butter melts and causes droopiness.

2. Line the crust with parchment paper. Add weights of your choosing to fill at least three-fourths full. You can use ceramic pie weights, dried beans, rice, or granulated sugar. Bake until the edges begin to look dry. Carefully remove the paper and weights. At this point it is "par-baked."

3. Return to the oven, and bake until fully baked. It should look completely dry on the sides and on the bottom and lightly golden all over.

CHAPTER 6

COOKIES & BARS

Are you looking for "just a bite of something sweet"? One, two, or even three of these cookies and bars will satisfy your sugar cravings and brighten up your day.

Chocolate Chip Cookies

Makes 36

Remember coming home from school to a wonderful smell, peeking in the cookie jar, and finding America's favorite variety?

1 cup unsalted butter, softened
1 cup firmly packed light brown sugar
½ cup granulated sugar
2 large eggs, lightly beaten, room temperature
2 teaspoons vanilla extract
3 cups White Lily All-Purpose Flour
1 teaspoon baking soda
½ teaspoon salt
1 (12-ounce) bag semisweet chocolate chips
1 cup chopped nuts (optional)

1. In a large bowl, beat butter and sugars with a mixer at medium speed until fluffy, 3 to 4 minutes, stopping to scrape sides of bowl. Beat in eggs and vanilla until light and fluffy.
2. In a medium bowl, stir together flour, baking soda, and salt. Add flour mixture to butter mixture all at once; beat at low speed just until combined. Stir in chocolate chips and nuts (if using). Refrigerate for at least 1 hour.
3. Preheat oven to 375°. Line baking sheets with parchment paper.
4. Using a 2-tablespoon spring-loaded scoop, scoop dough, and place 3 inches apart on prepared pans.
5. Bake until bottoms are golden brown, 8 to 10 minutes. Let cool on pans for 5 minutes. Remove from pans, and let cool completely on wire racks.

Kitchen Tip

After scooping the dough in step 4, place dough balls on a parchment paper-lined baking sheet and freeze until firm. Place frozen dough balls in a resealable plastic freezer bag. Freeze for up to 3 months. Take a few out to bake when you want warm cookies.

Pecan Sandies

Makes about 14

The perfect mix of sweetness and crunch, nothing says Southern like using pecans in your baked goods.

½ cup unsalted butter, room temperature*
¼ cup firmly packed light brown sugar
1¼ cups White Lily All-Purpose Flour
½ cup finely chopped pecans

1. Preheat oven to 350°. Line baking sheets with parchment paper.

2. In a large bowl, beat butter and brown sugar with a mixer at medium-low speed until creamy, about 3 minutes. Stir in flour and pecans just until combined. Shape into ball.

3. Turn out dough onto a lightly floured surface, and roll to ½-inch thickness. Using a 1¾-inch round cutter, cut dough, and place 2 inches apart on prepared pans.

4. Bake until edges are lightly browned, 15 to 20 minutes. Remove from pans, and let cool completely on wire racks.

*Unlike softened butter, room temperature butter should provide no resistance when pressed with a finger. At this point, the butter is softened enough to easily combine with your other ingredients.

Kitchen Tip

Even if you purchase prechopped pecans, make sure to give them another fine chop to get the pieces small and uniform.

Sugar Cookies

Makes 24

For late-night cravings, these simple treats are quick to throw together and easy to adapt into sandwich cookies.

½ cup unsalted butter, softened
1½ cups plus 3 tablespoons granulated sugar, divided
1 large egg, room temperature and lightly beaten
2 teaspoons vanilla extract
2⅓ cups White Lily All-Purpose Flour
½ teaspoon baking powder
½ teaspoon baking soda
½ teaspoon salt

1. In the bowl of a stand mixer fitted with the paddle attachment, beat butter and 1½ cups sugar at medium speed until fluffy, 3 to 4 minutes, stopping to scrape sides of bowl. Slowly add egg, beating until light in color and well combined and stopping to scrape sides of bowl.

2. In a medium bowl, whisk together flour, baking powder, and salt. Add flour mixture to butter mixture all at once, and beat at low speed just until combined, 1 to 2 minutes, stopping to scrape sides of bowl. Cover dough with plastic wrap, and refrigerate for 25 minutes.

3. Preheat oven to 350°. Line rimmed baking sheets with parchment paper.

4. In a small shallow dish, place remaining 3 tablespoons sugar.

5. Using a 2-tablespoon spring-loaded scoop, scoop dough, and gently roll into balls. Roll in sugar, and place at least 2½ inches apart on prepared pans.

6. Bake until edges are set and bottoms are light golden brown, 10 to 12 minutes. Let cool on pans for 5 minutes. Remove from pans, and let cool completely on wire racks.

Kitchen Tip

For delicious ice cream sandwiches, cut the baking time for these cookies by 1 to 2 minutes so the cookies are soft. Let cool completely on the pans. Place a scoop of your favorite ice cream on flat side of half of cookies. Place remaining cookies, flat side down, on top of ice cream. Wrap individually in plastic wrap, and freeze.

Rich Peanut Butter Bars

Makes 24

This chewy treat is White Lily's most-requested cookie recipe. It first appeared on flour bags more than 20 years ago.

½ cup creamy peanut butter
⅓ cup unsalted butter
1½ cups granulated sugar
1 cup White Lily Self-Rising Flour
2 large eggs, room temperature
1 teaspoon vanilla extract
Peanut Butter-Cream Cheese Frosting
    (recipe follows)
Melted bittersweet chocolate

1. Preheat oven to 350°. Spray a 13x9-inch baking pan with baking spray with flour.
2. In the top of a double boiler, combine peanut butter and butter. Cook over simmering water until melted. Transfer melted peanut butter mixture to a large bowl. Add sugar, flour, eggs, and vanilla, and stir until well combined. Spread batter in prepared pan.
3. Bake until a wooden pick inserted in center comes out with a few moist crumbs, 25 to 30 minutes. Let cool completely in pan. Spread Peanut Butter Cream Cheese Frosting on top, and drizzle with melted chocolate. Let stand until chocolate is set.

Peanut Butter-Cream Cheese Frosting

Makes 2 cups

1 cup cream cheese, softened
1 cup creamy peanut butter
½ cup confectioners' sugar
2 teaspoons vanilla extract

1. In the bowl of a stand mixer fitted with the paddle attachment, beat cream cheese and peanut butter at medium speed until smooth, 1½ to 2 minutes. With mixer on low speed, gradually add confectioners' sugar and vanilla. Increase mixer speed to medium-low, and beat until smooth. Use immediately.

Kitchen Tip

Fold chopped peanuts into your batter for an element of crunch.

Snickerdoodles

Makes 28

Sugar and spice and everything nice—that's what snickerdoodles are made of. Get ready for the comforting smell of cinnamon to waft through your home.

½ cup all-vegetable shortening, softened
1 cup plus 1½ tablespoons granulated sugar, divided
1 large egg, lightly beaten
½ teaspoon vanilla extract
2 cups sifted White Lily All-Purpose Flour
2 teaspoons baking powder
½ teaspoon salt
½ teaspoon ground cinnamon
1 large egg white

1. In a large bowl, beat shortening and 1 cup sugar with a mixer at medium speed until fluffy, 3 to 4 minutes, stopping to scrape sides of bowl. Beat in egg and vanilla.

2. In a medium bowl, sift together flour, baking powder, and salt. Add flour mixture to shortening mixture all at once, and beat at low speed just until combined. Turn out dough, and shape into 2 (7-inch) logs. Wrap in plastic wrap, and refrigerate for 1 hour.

3. Preheat oven to 350°. Line baking sheets with parchment paper.

4. In a small bowl, stir together cinnamon and remaining 1½ tablespoons sugar.

5. Working with 1 dough log at a time, slice into ½-inch-thick disks, and place 1 inch apart on prepared pans. Lightly brush with egg white, and sprinkle with cinnamon sugar.

6. Bake until light in color and bottoms are starting to take on color, 6 to 8 minutes. Sprinkle with remaining cinnamon sugar. Let cool on pans for 5 minutes. Remove from pans, and let cool completely on wire racks.

Kitchen Tip

Be sure to lightly brush the egg white on the dough for even coverage of the cinnamon sugar. If too much is brushed on, the cinnamon sugar forms clumps on the cookies, which gives them a crackled look after baking.

CHAPTER 7

BREADS

Loaves, rolls, crusts, doughnuts—yes, please!
Up your baking game and fall in love with the scent
of freshly baked bread warming your kitchen.

BREAD ESSENTIALS

Baking

To check if your bread is done, remove it from the pan and tap the bottom of the loaf. It should make a hollow sound and an instant-read thermometer inserted in the bread's center will register 205° for lean dough or 190° for enriched dough. Remove the bread from the pan, and let it cool on a wire rack.

Storage

Bread freezes very well. Freeze it whole or sliced by packing it into freezer bags or wrapping it in heavy-duty foil. It can be thawed at room temperature or heated in the oven, toaster, or toaster oven at 350°. You should never refrigerate bread, as refrigeration can cause bread to become stale more quickly than at room temperature.

Be sure your bread is completely cooled before covering it with plastic wrap. Homemade bread will last only a few days at room temperature, whereas the bread you buy at the store contains additives that keep it fresh. Homemade bread, however, tastes 10 times better.

Potato Pan Rolls

Makes 12

Serve them with soups, stews, or meat and threes. You won't be able to eat just one of these deliciously fluffy rolls.

- 4½ to 4¾ cups White Lily All-Purpose Flour, divided
- ¼ cup granulated sugar
- 1 (0.25-ounce) package active dry yeast
- 1½ teaspoons salt
- 1 cup whole milk
- ¼ cup plus 2 tablespoons unsalted butter, melted and divided
- ½ cup mashed potatoes (prepared without milk, butter, and seasonings), room temperature
- 2 large eggs, room temperature and divided
- Everything bagel seasoning

1. In the bowl of a stand mixer fitted with the paddle attachment, beat 1½ cups flour, sugar, yeast, and salt at low speed until combined.
2. In a medium saucepan, heat milk and ¼ cup melted butter over medium heat until an instant-read thermometer registers 120° to 130°. Add warm milk mixture to flour mixture; beat at medium-low speed for 2 minutes, stopping to scrape sides of bowl. Add mashed potatoes and 1 egg; beat at medium speed for 2 minutes. With mixer on low speed, gradually add 3 cups flour, beating just until combined.
3. Switch to the dough hook attachment. Beat at medium-low speed until a soft, smooth, elastic dough forms, 6 to 10 minutes; add up to remaining ¼ cup flour, 1 tablespoon at a time, if dough is too sticky. Test dough using the windowpane test. (See page 136.) Cover and let rise in a warm, draft-free place (75°) until doubled in size, 35 to 45 minutes.
4. Spray a 13x9-inch rimmed baking sheet with cooking spray. Line bottom of pan with parchment paper.
5. Punch down dough; cover and let stand for 5 minutes. Turn out dough onto a clean surface; divide into 12 portions, keeping dough covered as you work. On a clean surface, shape each portion into a ball (see tips on page 140). Place on prepared pan. Cover and let rise in a warm, draft-free place (75°) until doubled in size, 35 to 45 minutes. Use the finger dent test (see below) to determine if dough has risen enough.
6. Preheat oven to 375°.
7. In a small bowl, whisk remaining 1 egg. Brush tops of dough with egg.
8. Bake until golden brown and an instant-read thermometer inserted in center of a roll registers 190°, 15 to 18 minutes. Brush tops of warm rolls with remaining 2 tablespoons melted butter. Sprinkle with everything bagel seasoning. Serve warm.

Use the finger dent test:

We use the finger dent test to tell when a dough has been fully (correctly) proofed. This can be used after both the first and second rise. With a floured finger, poke or make a dent in proofed dough.
- If the dough fully springs back, it needs more time.
- If the dough springs back only slightly, the dough is ready.
- If the dough does not spring back at all, it is overproofed.

Everything bagel seasoning can be found in most grocery and specialty food stores on the spice aisle. It is a mixture of seeds (like sesame and poppy) and seasonings (like salt) commonly found on everything bagels sold in bagel shops and bakeries.

Glazed Cinnamon Rolls

Makes 12

*Your weekend called and asked for homemade cinnamon rolls. Eat them for breakfast and
maybe even sneak another for a late-night snack.*

5 to 5⅓ cups White Lily All-Purpose Flour, divided
⅓   cup granulated sugar
1   (0.25-ounce) package active dry yeast
1¼   teaspoons salt, divided
1¼   cups whole milk
½   cup unsalted butter
1   large egg, room temperature
¾   cup firmly packed light brown sugar
1½   tablespoons ground cinnamon
¼   teaspoon ground nutmeg
¼   cup unsalted butter, room temperature*
Sugar Glaze (recipe follows)

1. In the bowl of a stand mixer fitted with the paddle attachment, beat 1½ cups flour, granulated sugar, yeast, and 1 teaspoon salt at medium-low speed until well combined, stopping to scrape sides of bowl.

2. In a medium saucepan, heat milk and butter over medium heat until butter is melted and an instant-read thermometer registers 120° to 130°. Add warm milk mixture to flour mixture; beat at medium-low speed for 2 minutes, stopping to scrape sides of bowl. Add egg; beat at medium speed for 2 minutes. With mixer on low speed, gradually add 3½ cups flour, beating just until combined and stopping to scrape sides of bowl.

3. Switch to the dough hook attachment. Beat at medium-low speed until a soft, tacky dough forms, 6 to 10 minutes, stopping to scrape sides of bowl and dough hook; add up to remaining ⅓ cup flour, 1 tablespoon at a time, if dough is too sticky. (Dough should pass the windowpane test [see page 136] but may still stick slightly to sides of bowl.)

4. Spray a large bowl with cooking spray. Place dough in bowl, turning to grease top. Cover and let rise in a warm, draft-free place (75°) until doubled in size, 40 minutes to 1 hour.

5. Preheat oven to 375°. Spray a light metal 13x9-inch baking pan with cooking spray.

6. In a small bowl, stir together brown sugar, cinnamon, nutmeg, and remaining ¼ teaspoon salt.

7. Lightly punch down dough; cover and let stand for 5 minutes. Turn out dough onto a lightly floured surface, and roll into an 18x12-inch rectangle. Using a large offset spatula, spread room temperature butter onto dough, leaving a ½-inch border on one long side. Sprinkle evenly with brown sugar mixture. Starting with long side opposite border, roll dough into a log, pinching seam to seal. Gently shape log to 18 inches long with even thickness. Using a serrated knife dipped in flour, cut into 12 slices (about 1½ inches thick each), trimming edges slightly if necessary. Place rolls, cut side down, in prepared pan. Cover and let rise in a warm, draft-free place (75°) until doubled in size, 35 to 40 minutes.

8. Bake until lightly golden and an instant-read thermometer inserted in center registers at least 190°, 25 to 28 minutes, loosely covering with foil to prevent excess browning, if necessary. Let cool in pan for 10 minutes. Using a small offset spatula, spread Sugar Glaze over warm rolls. Serve warm.

*Unlike softened butter, room temperature butter should provide no resistance when pressed with a finger. At this point, the butter is softened enough to easily spread over dough.

Sugar Glaze
Makes about 1 cup

2½   cups confectioners' sugar
¼   cup whole milk
2   tablespoons unsalted butter, melted
⅛   teaspoon salt

1. In a medium bowl, stir together all ingredients until smooth and well combined. Use immediately.

White Loaf Bread

Makes 2 (8½x4½-inch) loaves

Whether you use it for thick-cut tomato sandwiches, generously buttered toast, or the ultimate addition to homemade soup, there are endless delicious options for a loaf of this white bread.

½ cup warm water (105° to 115°)
1 (0.25-ounce) package active dry yeast
1¾ cups whole milk
2 tablespoons granulated sugar
2 tablespoons all-vegetable shortening
2 teaspoons salt
5¾ to 6¼ cups White Lily Bread Flour, divided
Butter or margarine, melted

1. In a large bowl, stir together ½ cup warm water and yeast. Let stand until foamy, about 5 minutes.
2. In a medium saucepan, heat milk, sugar, shortening, and salt over medium heat until an instant-read thermometer registers 105° to 115°. Add warm milk mixture to yeast mixture, stirring until combined. Add 2½ cups flour, beating with a mixer at low speed just until combined. Stir in 3¼ cups flour; add up to remaining ½ cup flour, 1 tablespoon at a time, to make a fairly stiff dough.
3. Turn out dough onto a lightly floured surface, and knead for 10 minutes, adding flour, 1 tablespoon at a time, as needed to prevent sticking. Shape into a round.
4. Oil another large bowl. Place dough in bowl, turning to grease top. Cover with a clean, damp, lint-free towel, and let rise in a warm, draft-free place (75°) until doubled in size, about 1 hour.
5. Punch down dough. Turn out onto a lightly floured surface. Divide dough in half. Shape each half into a smooth ball. Cover with a clean, damp, lint-free towel. Let stand for 10 minutes.
6. Spray 2 (8½x4½-inch) loaf pans with cooking spray.
7. Flatten dough to release air bubbles. Roll each half into a 14x8-inch rectangle. Starting with one short side, roll up each rectangle, jelly roll style; seal seam and ends, and tuck ends under. Place, seam side down, in prepared pans. Let rise in a warm, draft-free place (75°) until doubled in size, about 1 hour.
8. Preheat oven to 375°.
9. Bake until deep golden brown, about 45 minutes, covering with foil after 30 minutes of baking to prevent excess browning. Remove from pans, and let cool completely on wire racks. Brush tops with melted butter or margarine.

Use the windowpane test:

To use the windowpane test to check dough for proper gluten development, lightly flour hands and pinch off (don't tear) a small piece of dough. Slowly pull the dough out from the center. If the dough is ready, you will be able to stretch it until it's thin and translucent like a windowpane. If the dough tears, it's not quite ready. Beat for 1 minute, and test again.

If you do not have a baking stone, you can bake the pizza on a baking sheet. Dust it with cornmeal before putting the dough on, and bake it in bottom third of your oven.

Pizza

Makes 1 (12-inch) pizza

Use this recipe for your foundation and, of course, customize to your liking. Your go-to flavor combinations will be perfectly complemented by this recipe.

1¼ to 1¾ cups White Lily Bread Flour, divided
1 teaspoon instant yeast
1 teaspoon granulated sugar
½ teaspoon salt
½ cup warm water (120° to 130°)
2 tablespoons olive oil
Yellow cornmeal, for dusting
Desired sauce and toppings

1. Position oven rack in bottom third of oven. Place pizza stone in cold oven. Preheat oven to 450°. Let stone heat for 1 hour before using.
2. In the bowl of a stand mixer, whisk together 1¼ cups flour, yeast, sugar, and salt. Add ½ cup warm water and 1 tablespoon oil; using the paddle attachment, beat at low speed just until combined. Switch to the dough hook attachment, and beat at low speed until dough is elastic and pulls away from sides and bottom of bowl, 3 to 4 minutes; add up to remaining ½ cup flour, 1 tablespoon at a time, if dough is too sticky.
3. Lightly oil a medium bowl. Place dough in bowl, turning to grease top. Cover and let rise in a warm, draft-free place (75°) until doubled in size, 25 to 35 minutes.
4. Place a rimmed baking sheet upside down, and heavily dust with cornmeal. (Alternatively, heavily dust a flat baking sheet with cornmeal.)
5. Punch down dough; let stand for 5 minutes. Turn out onto a lightly floured surface, and stretch into a 12-inch circle. Place on prepared pan. Brush dough with remaining 1 tablespoon oil. Top with favorite sauce and toppings, leaving a ½-inch border around edges. Slide pizza directly onto hot pizza stone.
6. Bake until crust and bottom are golden and cheese (if using) is melted, 12 to 15 minutes. Let cool for 5 minutes. Serve hot.

Freezing dough:

1. Proceed with recipe through step 3. Punch down dough, and shape into a round. Immediately wrap in a double layer of plastic wrap, and place in a resealable plastic freezer bag. Freeze for up to 1 month.
2. To thaw: Unwrap and place in a large bowl. Cover and let thaw in refrigerator overnight. Before stretching dough, let stand, covered, at room temperature for 30 to 45 minutes.

Feather-Light Dinner Rolls

Makes 30

We call them "feather-light" for a reason: they melt in your mouth!

½ cup warm water (105° to 115°)
2 (0.25-ounce) packages active dry yeast
1½ cups whole milk
½ cup granulated sugar
¼ cup all-vegetable shortening
2 teaspoons salt
1 large egg, lightly beaten, room temperature
5¾ cups White Lily Bread Flour
Melted butter, for brushing

1. In the bowl of a stand mixer, stir together ½ cup warm water and yeast. Let stand until foamy, about 5 minutes.
2. In a medium saucepan, heat milk, sugar, shortening, and salt over medium heat until an instant-read thermometer registers 115°. Add warm milk mixture to yeast mixture. Stir in egg. Add 3 cups flour; using the paddle attachment, beat at low speed until dough is fairly smooth, about 3 minutes.
3. Switch to the dough hook attachment. Add 2½ cups flour, and beat at low speed until a very soft dough forms. Slowly add remaining ¼ cup flour, as needed, until a very soft dough forms, about 10 minutes. Shape into a ball.
4. Spray a large bowl with cooking spray. Place dough in bowl, turning to grease top. Cover with a damp cloth or plastic wrap, and let rise in a warm, draft-free place (75°) until doubled in size, about 1 hour.
5. Butter 2 (13x9-inch) baking pans.
6. Punch down dough. Turn out onto a lightly floured surface. Divide dough into 30 portions. Shape into balls, and place in prepared pans. Cover with a damp cloth or plastic wrap, and let rise in a warm, draft-free place (75°) until doubled in size, about 45 minutes.
7. Preheat oven to 400°.
8. Bake until golden brown, 13 to 15 minutes. Brush tops with melted butter. Serve hot or let cool.

There are two ways to shape a roll:

1. Hold one portion of dough between your fingertips with one hand. Using the other hand, pinch dough using your thumb and forefinger, and pull down, pinching at the bottom. Rotate dough, and continue to pinch and pull until dough becomes a smooth, tight ball.
2. Place one portion of dough on a very lightly floured surface. Using your palm, press down on dough to release any air bubbles. Then start to rotate your hand until dough starts to form a ball; turn your hand, and make a "C" shape. Keep dough under your palm, and continue rotating your hand and applying pressure in same direction until dough becomes a smooth, tight ball.

Banana Nut Bread

Makes 2 (8½x4½-inch) loaves

Slice and spread with cream cheese or butter for picnics and snacks.

3½ cups White Lily All-Purpose Flour
2 teaspoons baking powder
1 teaspoon baking soda
½ teaspoon salt
3 cups mashed ripe banana (5 to 6 bananas)
2⅓ cups granulated sugar
1 cup unsalted butter, melted
4 large eggs, lightly beaten, room temperature
1 teaspoon vanilla extract
1 cup chopped walnuts, black walnuts, or pecans
Softened butter, to serve

1. Preheat oven to 325°. Spray 2 (8½x4½-inch) loaf pans with baking spray with flour.
2. In a medium bowl, whisk together flour, baking powder, baking soda, and salt.
3. In a large bowl, whisk together banana, sugar, melted butter, eggs, and vanilla until well combined. Slowly add flour mixture to banana mixture, stirring just until moistened. Fold in nuts. Divide batter between prepared pans. (Pans will be full, but batter will not overflow.)
4. Bake until a wooden pick inserted in center comes out clean, 1 hour to 1 hour and 10 minutes, covering with foil to prevent excess browning, if necessary. Let cool in pans for 10 minutes. Remove from pans, and let cool completely on a wire rack. Serve with softened butter.

Sourdough Bread

Makes 1 boule

After you've mastered the White Loaf Bread, it's time to take on sourdough. Just as delicious but different in flavor and texture, with this bread, your sandwiches will never be the same.

Leaven:
- 6 tablespoons lukewarm water (80°)
- 1 tablespoon sourdough starter
- ⅔ cup White Lily Bread Flour

Dough:
- 1 cup plus 2 tablespoons lukewarm water (80°)
- 3½ cups White Lily Bread Flour, divided
- 1½ teaspoons salt

1. For leaven: In a medium bowl, stir together 6 tablespoons lukewarm water and sourdough culture. Add flour, and stir thoroughly by hand until smooth and no dry bits of flour remain. Loosely cover bowl, and let stand at room temperature overnight.

2. For dough: In the bowl of a stand mixer fitted with the dough hook attachment, place leaven and 1 cup plus 2 tablespoons lukewarm water. Add 3¼ cups flour and salt. Beat at low speed, slowly adding remaining ¼ cup flour. Beat until dough comes together and does not tear easily when pulled, 6 to 7 minutes. (Dough will not be smooth.)

3. Lightly spray a large bowl with cooking spray. Place dough in bowl. Cover and let rise in a warm, draft-free place (75°) until dough feels smooth and soft, 2½ to 3 hours, turning every 30 minutes. (To complete a turn, grab underside of dough, stretch it up, and fold it to center of dough. Do this 4 times around bowl. See pages 146 and 147.)

4. Turn out dough onto a lightly floured surface. Using just your fingertips dipped in flour, gently press dough into a 1-inch-thick oval. Fold one third over center; fold remaining third over first fold. Cover with a kitchen towel, and let dough stand for 20 to 30 minutes.

5. For final shape, press dough out again using your fingertips; grab bottom edge, and gently stretch and fold bottom third over center third. Stretch right side out, and fold right third over center; repeat with left side. Finish by folding top third over previous folds. Roll loaf away from you, to seam side down, and using both hands, cup dough and pull it toward you to seal. Turn dough 90 degrees, and pull again. Repeat until a tight, smooth boule forms. Place in a banneton (proofing basket) or a medium bowl lined with a kitchen towel heavily dusted with flour. Let rise in a warm, draft-free place (75°) for 3 hours. (Alternatively, refrigerate to cold-ferment overnight. Let stand at room temperature for 1 hour before baking).

6. Place a Dutch oven with lid in cold oven. Preheat oven to 500°.

7. Turn boule out of banneton or bowl onto a piece of parchment paper lightly dusted with flour. Using a lame or sharp paring knife, score top of loaf. Carefully remove Dutch oven from oven, and place boule in Dutch oven. Place lid on Dutch oven, and return to oven.

8. Immediately reduce oven temperature to 425°. Bake for 25 minutes. Remove lid, and bake until bread is deep golden brown and an instant-read thermometer inserted in center registers 205°, 5 to 10 minutes more. Immediately remove from Dutch oven, and let cool completely on a wire rack.

How to make a sourdough starter:

The starter is flour and water that have gone through the process of fermentation, which is when good bacteria and wild yeast that are present develop structure, flavor, and leavening.

Day 1: Mix ¾ cup room temperature water and 1⅓ cups White Lily Bread Flour with your hands in a glass bowl or large glass jar until smooth. It will have a thick, paste-like consistency. Cover with a kitchen towel and place in a cool place out of direct sunlight.

Day 3: After two to three days of rest, there should be some activity, mostly bubbles of carbon dioxide and a faint tangy smell. There should be a slightly discolored skin on the surface. Remove the skin, and begin discarding and feeding once a day. How to feed: Every day around the same time, discard about ¾ of the starter and then refresh it with 6 tablespoons room temperature water and ⅔ cup bread flour. Don't fret if you forget to feed it one day; just make sure you feed it the next.

Day 5: At this point, the sourdough culture should be showing significant activity with a noticeable sour smell and plenty of air pockets. In two weeks, it'll begin to rise and fall on a regular basis—this is considered a healthy starter ready to use.

How to make a perfect sourdough boule:

1. Begin with your sourdough starter. Remove 1 tablespoon of sourdough starter before you feed it, and place it in a separate bowl. Feed your starter as normal for future bread making. With the 1 tablespoon of starter, add the lukewarm water and flour as listed in the recipe. This is your leaven (or levain) that needs to sit overnight to mature.

2. This dough is different than others in this book. You are not looking for a smooth, fully kneaded dough here. Look for the dough to be elastic, which means when you pinch the dough with floured fingers and start to pull the dough, it doesn't tear easily. This dough also has a high hydration, which means it will be sticky. Resist the urge to add more flour.

3.–5. Once in the bowl, let it rise for 2½ to 3 hours while completing a series of turns or folds. To complete one turn or fold, start by preparing your hands. (Some people flour their hands, some people dip them in water, and some people oil their hands.) Then reach one hand under the dough, stretch up, and fold it back over the rest of the dough in the center. Repeat this three more times around the bowl. This develops gluten and creates a smooth, strong final dough.

6. Once your dough is ready, turn out onto a lightly floured surface. Using just your fingertips so you don't press out all the air pockets, press into a 1-inch-thick oval.

7. Fold dough into thirds, lightly flour, cover, and let rest for 20 or 30 minutes. This is called a bench rest, and the purpose of it is to preshape the dough and let the gluten relax some, making the final shape easier.

8. For the final shape, a boule, press the dough out again into an 1-inch-thick oval using just your fingertips. Stretch and fold the bottom edge, the one closest to you, to the center.

9. Stretch and fold in the sides to the center.

10. Finish by grabbing the top edge, stretching, and folding over the other fold to the center. Roll the loaf over so it is seam side down. Using both hands, cup the dough and pull it toward you to seal. Turn dough 90 degrees (quarter turn), and pull again. Repeat this as many times as needed until a tight, smooth boule forms. Note: if you only have an oval dutch oven, rotate the dough 180 degrees between pulling until it creates a tight, smooth oval, or batard.

11. After it rises in a bowl lined with a floured kitchen towel, turn out onto lightly floured parchment paper to score the bread. Scoring the bread gives a defined place for air to escape. It can be done with a razor, a lame, or a sharp paring knife.

12. Carefully place in the preheated Dutch oven and cover with a lid that fits well. The steam should stay trapped in the Dutch oven so a crust forms.

Doughnuts
Makes 10

Whip up a delicious batch of fresh cinnamon-flavored doughnuts in your own kitchen.

1 cup warm whole milk (110° to 115°)
1 cup plus 6 tablespoons granulated sugar, divided
1 (0.25-ounce) package active dry yeast
¼ cup unsalted butter, melted and cooled for 10 minutes
2 large eggs, room temperature
2¼ cups White Lily All-Purpose Flour, plus more for dusting
2 cups White Lily Bread Flour
1 teaspoon salt
1 teaspoon apple pie spice
Vegetable oil or canola oil, for frying
2 teaspoons ground cinnamon

1. In a large bowl, whisk together warm milk, 1 tablespoon sugar, and yeast. Let stand until foamy, 5 to 10 minutes.
2. Add melted butter and eggs to yeast mixture, whisking until combined. Add flours, 5 tablespoons sugar, salt, and pie spice. Using a spatula or wooden spoon, stir until a shaggy dough forms. Turn out dough onto a lightly floured surface. Using floured hands, flatten dough until about 1 inch thick. Fold dough in half toward you; using the heels of your hands, push dough away. Turn 90 degrees, and repeat folding and turning until smooth and elastic, 4 to 5 minutes, lightly re-flouring surface and hands as needed.
3. Spray a large bowl with cooking spray. Place dough in bowl, turning to grease top. Cover and let rise in a warm, draft-free place (75°) until doubled in size, about 1 hour. (Alternatively, cover and let rise in refrigerator overnight. When ready to use, proceed as directed.)
4. Cut out 10 (4-inch) squares of parchment paper, and place on 2 large baking sheets. Spray parchment with cooking spray.
5. Punch down dough; turn out onto a heavily floured surface, and roll to ½-inch thickness. Using a 3½-inch doughnut cutter dipped in flour, cut dough. Gently transfer to prepared parchment squares, spacing at least 1½ inches apart. Reroll scraps, and let stand for 5 to 10 minutes; cut scraps. Cover and let rise in a warm, draft-free place (75°) until puffed, about 30 minutes.
6. In a large Dutch oven, pour oil to a depth of 2 inches, and heat over medium heat until a deep-fry thermometer registers 365° to 375°.
7. Line large rimmed baking sheets with paper towels.
8. In a medium bowl, stir together cinnamon and remaining 1 cup sugar.
9. Working in batches, use parchment paper to gently pick up doughnuts, and add to oil. Remove parchment from oil using tongs. Fry until golden brown, 45 seconds to 1 minute per side. Using a spider strainer, remove doughnuts, and let drain on prepared pans. Place 1 doughnut in cinnamon sugar, tossing to coat. Place on a wire rack. Repeat with remaining doughnuts. Serve warm or at room temperature.

Hand kneading for doughnuts and more!

1. After adding all ingredients to the bowl, begin stirring together until you reach a shaggy dough, meaning the majority of flour has been incorporated but the dough is still textured and tacky.
2. Place dough on a lightly floured surface, and flour your hands. (Note: You will need to re-flour your hands and the work surface a lot in the beginning and sparingly toward the end.) Flatten dough to about 1-inch thickness to start. Fold dough in half toward you.
3. Using the heel of your hand, push dough away from you.
4. Turn dough 90 degrees (or a quarter turn) and repeat the motion until dough is smooth and elastic. To know when dough is fully kneaded, use the windowpane test (page 136).

CHAPTER 8

FROM THE VAULT

For something nostalgic and never disappointing,
we've gathered some of our favorite classics that you'll
want to add to your everyday recipe rotation.

Best-Ever White Lily Waffles

Makes about 3 servings

Waffles are for those who want ridges to hold their syrup in place.
This recipe will provide perfection every time.

1   cup White Lily Self-Rising Flour
½   teaspoon baking soda
1   cup whole buttermilk, room temperature
⅓   cup unsalted butter, melted
2   large eggs, separated, room temperature
Maple syrup, fresh raspberries, and whipped
    cream, to serve

1. Heat waffle iron according to manufacturer's instructions.
2. In a medium bowl, stir together flour and baking soda.
3. In another medium bowl, stir together buttermilk, melted butter, and egg yolks. Add buttermilk mixture to flour mixture, stirring just until combined.
4. In a small bowl, beat egg whites with a mixer at high speed until stiff peaks form. Fold egg whites into batter in three additions.
5. Spray waffle iron with cooking spray. Pour about ½ cup batter in center of lower half of waffle iron for 1 (5x4-inch) waffle. Cook until no steam shows around edges, about 4 minutes. Using a fork, gently loosen waffle. Repeat with remaining batter. Serve immediately with maple syrup, raspberries, and whipped cream.

Kitchen Tip

For a fun variation, top waffles with yogurt and fresh berries. For a dessert waffle, try frozen strawberry yogurt and banana slices. Or sprinkle 2 tablespoons pecans over batter after pouring in waffle iron. Dust waffles with nutmeg, if desired.

Cheddar Cheese Wafers

Makes about 50

Cookies are supposed to be sweet, but this tangy, tasty snack is a traditional favorite at Southern teas and weddings. If you have a cookie press, you can make these wafers into fancy, ridged shapes. But other quick and easy shapes are provided here, too.

1½   cups White Lily All-Purpose Flour
¼   teaspoon ground red pepper
2   cups shredded Cheddar cheese, room temperature
½   cup unsalted butter, softened
¼   teaspoon salt

1. Preheat oven to 375°. Line a baking sheet with parchment paper.

2. In a medium bowl, stir together flour and red pepper.

3. In the work bowl of a food processor, place cheese, butter, and salt; process until smooth. Add flour mixture, and process until smooth. Refrigerate until firm enough to roll, 20 to 30 minutes.

4. Turn out dough onto a lightly floured surface, and roll into a ¼-inch-thick square. Trim edges, and cut square into 2x1-inch strips. Place ½ inch apart on prepared pan. (Alternatively, make straws using a cookie press with a star attachment.)

5. Bake until edges are lightly browned, 9 to 11 minutes.

Kitchen Tip

For Cheddar cheese crackers, shape the prepared dough into 2-inch-thick logs, and refrigerate for 1 hour.

Old-Fashioned Pound Cake

Makes 2 (8½x4½-inch) cakes

This famous cake is based on the original—it contains 1 pound of each ingredient, hence the name. Originally, it took two hours to make by hand, but thankfully hand and stand mixers make the work easier for modern bakers.

1 pound salted butter (2 cups), softened
1 pound granulated sugar (2¼ cups)
1 pound eggs (about 9 large eggs), room temperature
1 teaspoon vanilla extract
½ teaspoon lemon extract
1 pound sifted White Lily All-Purpose Flour (4½ cups)
½ teaspoon baking powder (optional)
Fresh strawberries and whipped cream, to serve

1. Preheat oven to 325°. Spray 2 (8½x4½-inch) loaf pans with cooking spray. Line pans with parchment paper, letting excess extend over sides of pans.

2. In the bowl of a stand mixer fitted with the paddle attachment, beat butter and sugar at medium speed until fluffy and smooth, 5 to 7 minutes, stopping to scrape sides of bowl. Add eggs, one at a time, beating until well combined after each addition. Beat in extracts.

3. In a large bowl, whisk together flour and baking powder (if using). With mixer on low speed, gradually add flour mixture to butter mixture, beating just until combined after each addition and stopping to scrape sides of bowl. Divide batter between prepared pans.

4. Bake until golden brown and cake starts pulling away from edges, 1 hour and 15 minutes to 1 hour and 25 minutes, covering with foil after 45 minutes of baking to prevent excess browning. Let cool in pans for 15 minutes. Using excess parchment as handles, remove from pans, and let cool completely on a wire rack. Serve with strawberries and whipped cream.

Caramel Cookies

Makes about 56

*This simple recipe was recommended for bridge luncheons in the 1900s
White Lily cookbook for "fine baking."*

3   cups White Lily All-Purpose Flour
1½   teaspoons cream of tartar
1   teaspoon baking soda
2   cups firmly packed light brown sugar
½   cup all-vegetable shortening
2   large eggs, room temperature and beaten

1. In a large bowl, sift together flour, cream of tartar, and baking soda. Stir in brown sugar. Using a pastry cutter or 2 forks, cut in shortening. Slowly stir in eggs.

2. Turn out dough onto a cutting board, and knead well. Shape into 2 (7-inch) logs, wrap in plastic wrap, and refrigerate overnight.

3. Preheat oven to 400°. Line baking sheets with parchment paper.

4. Using a sharp knife, cut dough crosswise into ¼-inch-thick slices, and place 1½ inches apart on prepared pans.

5. Bake until edges are lightly golden, 6 to 7 minutes. Let cool on pans for 2 minutes. Remove from pans, and let cool completely on wire racks.

Pick-a-Piece Biscuit Loaf

Makes 1 (8½x4½-inch) loaf

Orange Honey Butter makes this recipe sweet and tangy while its shape and texture makes it perfect for sharing and enjoying.

5   cups White Lily Self-Rising Flour
¼   cup granulated sugar
½   teaspoon salt
1½   cups cold unsalted butter, cubed
1½   cups cold whole buttermilk
Orange Honey Butter (recipe on page 32), divided
Orange Sugar Glaze (recipe follows)

1. Preheat oven to 375°. Spray an 8½x4½-inch loaf pan with cooking spray.
2. In a large bowl, whisk together flour, sugar, and salt. Using a pastry blender or 2 forks, cut in cold butter until mixture is crumbly. Add cold buttermilk, stirring just until dry ingredients are moistened.
3. On a lightly floured surface, gently knead dough until it comes together. Roll to ¼-inch thickness. Using a 3½-inch round cutter, cut dough into 16 rounds, rerolling scraps as necessary. Reserve 1 round. Brush top of remaining rounds with ¼ cup Orange Honey Butter.
4. Stand prepared pan vertically on one short side; starting at bottom of pan, carefully layer rounds, Orange Honey Butter side up, one on top of the other, in a zigzag pattern. Top with reserved plain round. Turn pan upright onto its bottom.

5. Bake until top and sides are golden, about 1 hour and 15 minutes, loosely covering with foil after 45 minutes of baking to prevent excess browning. Let cool in pan for 15 minutes. Remove from pan, and brush with 1 tablespoon Orange Honey Butter. Drizzle with Sugar Glaze. Serve warm or at room temperature with remaining Orange Honey Butter.

Orange Sugar Glaze
Makes about ½ cup

1½   cups confectioners' sugar, sifted
2½   tablespoons fresh orange juice, divided

1. In a small bowl, whisk together confectioners' sugar and 2 tablespoons orange juice until smooth. Stir in remaining ½ tablespoon orange juice if necessary to thin glaze. Use immediately.

Kitchen Tip

Freeze the dough rounds until slightly firm to make them easier to stack in the pan. This can also make it easier to rearrange the slices a bit if needed.

RECIPE INDEX

Biscuits
Cathead Biscuits 26
Flaky Layer Buttermilk Biscuits 22
Garlic Cheese Biscuits 21
Pick-a-Piece Biscuit Loaf 161
White Lily "Light" Biscuits 18

Biscuit Add-Ins and Toppings
Bacon Ranch Add-In 16
Blueberry and Honey Add-In 16
Cinnamon Molasses Butter 32
Garlic Butter 32
Grandma's Gravy 30
Lemon Basil Add-In 16
Mustard and Chive Add-In 16
Orange Honey Butter 32
Pimiento Cheese Add-In 16

Breads
Banana Nut Bread 143
Best-Ever White Lily Waffles 153
Cornmeal Pancakes 48
Doughnuts 149
Feather-Light Dinner Rolls 140
Glazed Cinnamon Rolls 135
Potato Pan Rolls 132
Scones 25
Sourdough Bread 144
White Loaf Bread 136

Cakes
Angel Food Cake 87
Brown Sugar Cinnamon Coffee Cake 88
Chocolate Layer Cake with Chocolate Silk Frosting 81
Cream Cheese Pound Cake 95
Old-Fashioned Pound Cake 157
Pineapple Upside-Down Cake 92
Southern Caramel Cake 91
Red Velvet Cake 78
The White Lily Cake 82

Cookies
Caramel Cookies 158
Chocolate Chip Cookies 118
Pecan Sandies 121
Rich Peanut Butter Bars 125
Snickerdoodles 126
Sugar Cookies 122

Cornbread
Creamy Corn Spoon Bread 51
Southwestern-Style Cornbread 47
White Lily Southern Cornbread 40

Frostings, Glazes, and Toppings
Caramel Frosting 91
Chocolate Silk Frosting 81
Cream Cheese Frosting 78
Orange Sugar Glaze 161
Peanut Butter-Cream Cheese Frosting 125
Pecan Streusel 88
Strawberry Glaze 87
Sugar Glaze 135
Sweetened Whipped Cream 87
White Buttercream Frosting 82
Yogurt Glaze 88

Pies and Fruit Desserts
Blueberry Muffins with Streusel Topping 107
Cherry Cobbler 108
Flaky Piecrust 101
Lemon Meringue Pie 115
Old-Fashioned Apple Pie 102
Peach Cobbler with Biscuit Topping 29
Peach Hand Pies 111
Strawberry Shortcakes 112

Savory Favorites
Barbecue Chicken Cornbread Bake 71
Buttermilk-Battered Chicken Tenders 68
Cheddar Cheese Wafers 154
Chicken and Dumplings with Vegetables 56
Chicken Pot Pie 60
Cornbread-Sausage Dressing 44
Cornmeal-Breaded Catfish 43
Country-Fried Steak with Gravy 59
Fresh Tomato Salsa 52
Homemade Hot Tamales 52
Hush Puppies 43
Pizza 139
Sausage, Egg, and Cheese Biscuit Casserole 72
Spicy Nashville Fried Chicken 63
Tomato Pie 64
White Chicken Chili Pot Pie 67

NOTES